AF560717

Education and Human Rights

EDUCATION AND HUMAN RIGHTS

By

Dr. M. Lakshmi Narasaiah
M.A., Ph.D.

Professor & Head
Department of Economics
Sri Krishnadevaraya University Post-graduate Centre
Kurnool–518 002
Andhra Pradesh (India)

DISCOVERY PUBLISHING HOUSE
NEW DELHI

Reprinted - 2017

ISBN: 978-81-7141-798-8

Education and Human Rights

Published by:

DISCOVERY PUBLISHING HOUSE PVT. LTD.
4383/4B, Ansari Road, Darya Ganj
New Delhi-110 002 (India)
Phone: +91-11-23279245, 43596064-65
Fax: +91-11-23253475
E-mail: discoverypublishinghouse@gmail.com
sales@discoverypublishinggroup.com
web: www.discoverypublishinggroup.com

Printed at:
Infinity Imaging Systems
Delhi

Preface

In contrast to the food supply challenge posed by the coming wave of population growth, the global need for teachers and classrooms will rise very slowly in the next half-century. In many countries, the school-age population is increasing much less rapidly than the overall national population. The trend illustrates that growth rates typically differ for different age strata of the population. It also shows that declining birth rates can take decades to move through an entire population.

At the global level, for example, total population is projected to increase by 54 per cent between 2000 and 2050, but the number of children aged 5 to 14 will grow by only 6 per cent. And of the world's largest countries-accounting for 60 per cent of global population in 1995-will actually begin to see decreases in the number of children aged 5 to 14 by 2015; for several of these countries, the decline in this age group has already begun. These countries will need fewer classrooms and teachers to educate the youngest members of society (assuming they maintain current class size and student-teacher ratios).

Plenty of nations, however, still have increasing child-age populations. Where countries have not acted to stabilize population, the base of the national population pyramid continues to expand, and pressures on the educational system will be severe. In the world's 10 fastest-growing countries, for example, most of which are in Africa and the Middle East, the child-age population will increase in average 93 per cent over the next half-century. Africa as a whole will see its school-age population grow by 75 per cent through 2040.

The rapid growth in African populations is especially worrisome because of the extra burden it imposes in a region already lagging in education. Only 56 per cent of Africans south of the Sahara are literate, compared with 71 per cent for all developing countries. Few African countries have universal primary education, and secondary education reaches only 4-5 per cent of African children. Educating today's children is challenge enough; the addition of another three students for every four already there will require heroic investments in education. But the alternative is grim: without additional investments in education, today's average student-teacher ratio of 42 in sub-Saharan Africa will reach 75 by 2040.

Many countries will be challenged to increase funding for education while ensuring that other worthy sectors also receive the support they need. With 900 million illiterate adults in the world, the case for a renewed commitment to education is easy to make. But competiting for these funds are the 840 million chronically hungry and the 1.2 billion without access to a decent toilet.

The budget stresses on governments attempting to meet these basic needs would clearly be reduced with smaller populations. Mozambique and Lesotho, for example, both met the UNESCO benchmark for investment in education in 1992-6 per cent of gross domestic product-and the two countries economies were roughly equal in size. Yet because Mozambique has many times the population of Lesotho, spending per child in Lesotho is about nine times higher than in Mozambique. For the majority of countries who do not meet the UNESCO funding standard, many of whom also fall short in providing other basic services, a decline in population pressure could help substantially to meet all of their social goals.

If national education systems begin to stress life-long learning for a rapidly changing world, as recommended by a 1998 UNESCO report on education in the twenty-first century, then extensive provision for adult education will be necessary, affecting even those countries with shrinking child-age populations, Such a development means that countries that started population stabilization programs earliest will be in the best position to educate their entire citizenry.

Dr. M. Lakshmi Narasaiah

Contents

1

For a Broader Approach to Education

In our rapidly changing world, literacy should be seen as an important evolutionary variable in every society. For the further a society progresses, the more it needs to adjust and adapt to new demands and pressures, so that literacy is lifelong necessity for all.

Literacy, in the broad sense, is the foundation for life skills, ranging from basic oral and written communication to the ability to solve scientific and social problems. Today it involves much more than the acquisition of 3 Rs. And a limited set of traditional skills. It is linked with the changing demands of life in a given socio-cultural context.

This means that local communities should be fully involved in defining the content of literacy programmes. The local dimension of literacy is extremely important, not only for accommodating the real needs of learners, but also for taking into account the linguistic and cultural realities of multicultural societies. For in the end, only the learners actually decide what they need to learn.

Building Bridges Between Cultures

Most literacy specialist have accepted this broader, more dynamic and culturally sensitive stance. It marks a long overdue acknowledgement of the positive role that local language and cultures can play in removing some of the serious pedagogical and psychological hurdles often encountered by learners, it is the only way to ensure the relevance and authority of literacy work.

Any one can insist here on the importance of multilingual education. Today education is as much about learning to live together as learning to know, to do and to be. Yet we cannot live together if our possibilities of expression are limited to a single linguistic frame. This is often at the root of problems encountered in multicultural societies. Of course, inequality in all its forms is a major factor. But internal conflicts often have purely cultural causes. It is more difficult for people to forge links with each other when they cannot communicate linguistically.

Yet children learn languages easily—much more so than the adults who take the decisions. We need to take much greater advantage of this fact. Children are expected to store too much information in their "hard memory"-much of it frankly useless! Giving them language skills provides them with bridges between cultures, enabling them to grow up without the debilitating sense that other cultures are lien. It is our task to try to ensure that education at all levels, and particularly basic education, promotes multilinguilism. And we must invest in such education, since to do so is to invest in peace.

It is also important to remind ourselves that literacy is not a neutral process which can be applied in all situations, all the time, regardless of social and economic realities. Such a narrow concept of literacy ignores its critical role as a tool of empowerment. One can treat adult learners as empty vessels waiting to be filled with predetermined bodies of knowledge disconnected from their social experience. Literacy must provide space of intellectual development, motivations for learning and a sense of self-esteem, if it is to be a genuine education for empowerment.

Bringing Adult Education into the Mainstream

Many individuals and families around the world are facing unexpected changes in the pattern of their daily lives, disrupting their plans for the future. The demands on educational services are increasing dramatically, especially in countries where the state is the main provider of education for children and adults. In today's world, we cannot afford a short-sighted approach which, in effect, excludes adult education from the mainstream of the education system, even after the concept of lifelong learning has been accepted as a framework for educational policy.

Literacy programmes must be given the priority they deserve. Lifelong learning for all requires quality adult education and literacy programmes with qualified personnel, relevant teaching programmes, appropriate post-literacy materials and decent facilities. We must ask ourselves whether we recently are prepared to make the necessary; Investments in adult education and literacy to ensure universal access to the types of programmes needed to reach the targets of education for all.

If we truly believe in lifelong learning, and if we seriously believe in redressing the balance of learning in our societies, then we should seek to develop in every country an open and more enabling system of education, breaking with past concepts of education as something which happens to people between the ages of six and twenty and which only the privileged of few were entitled to. Synergy has to be created between formal and non-formal education programmes.

A case in point is the family literacy concept. We all know that the continuing education of parents, particularly when they are illiterate or under-educated, can contribute very effectively to their children's success in school. In fact the family literacy approach is one of the most effective ways of breaking the cycle of inter-generational illiteracy. Education and training policies should include all types of learning, whether it takes place in a school, in the workplace or at home. There should be more innovation and creativity in using methods and approaches.

2

Population Growth and Education

In contrast to the food supply challenge posed by the coming wave of population growth, the global need for teachers and classrooms will rise very slowly in the next half-century. In many countries, the school-age population is increasing much less rapidly than the overall national population. The trend illustrates that growth rates typically differ for different age strata of the population. It also shows that declining birth rates can take decades to move through an entire population.

At the global level, for example, total population is projected to increase by 54 per cent between 2000 and 2050, but the number of children aged 5 to 14 will grow by only 6 per cent. And of the world's largest countries-accounting for 60 per cent of global population in 1995-will actually begin to see decreases in the number of children aged 5 to 14 by 2015; for several of these countries, the decline in this age group has already begun. These countries will need fewer classrooms and teachers to educate the youngest members of society (assuming they maintain current class size and student-teacher ratios).

Plenty of nations, however, still have increasing child-age populations. Where countries have not acted to stabilize population, the base of the national population pyramid continues to expand, and pressures on the educational system will be severe. In the world's 10 fastest-growing countries, for example, most of which are in Africa and the Middle East, the child-age population will increase in average 93 per cent over the next half-century. Africa as a whole will see its school-age population grow by 75 per cent through 2040.

The rapid growth in African populations is especially worrisome because of the extra burden it imposes in a region already lagging in education. Only 56 per cent of Africans south of the Sahara are literate, compared with 71 per cent for all developing countries. Few African countries have universal primary education, and secondary education reaches only 4-5 per cent of African children. Educating today's children is challenge enough; the addition of another three students for every four already there will require heroic investments in education. But the alternative is grim: without additional investments in education, today's average student-teacher ratio of 42 in sub-Saharan Africa will reach 75 by 2040.

Many countries will be challenged to increase funding for education while ensuring that other worthy sectors also receive the support they need. With 900 million illiterate adults in the world, the case for a renewed commitment to education is easy to make. But competiting for these funds are the 840 million chronically hungry and the 1.2 billion without access to a decent toilet.

The budget stresses on governments attempting to meet these basic needs would clearly be reduced with smaller populations. Mozambique and Lesotho, for example, both met the UNESCO benchmark for investment in education in 1992-6 per cent of gross domestic product-and the two countries economies were roughly equal in size. Yet because Mozambique has many times the population of Lesotho, spending per child in Lesotho is about nine times higher than in Mozambique. For the majority of countries who do not meet the UNESCO funding standard, many of whom also fall short in providing other basic services, a decline in population pressure could help substantially to meet all of their social goals.

If national education systems begin to stress life-long learning for a rapidly changing world, as recommended by a 1998 UNESCO report on education in the twenty-first century, then extensive provision for adult education will be necessary, affecting even those countries with shrinking child-age populations, Such a devèlopment means that countries that started population stabilization programmes earliest will be in the best position to educate their entire citizenry.

3

Private Education: The Poor's Best Chance?

Across the developing world, private schools and education companies are not only flourishing, but reaching the poor. India is a case in point. A Common assumption about the private sector in education is that it caters only to the elite, and that its promotion only serves to exacerbate inequality. On the contrary recent research points in the opposite direction. If we want to help some of the most disadvantages groups in society, then encouraging deeper private sector involvements is likely to be the best way forward.

Several developments are underway in India, all of which involve the private education sector meeting the needs of the poor in distinct ways. But India is not unique in this respect—similar phenomena are happening all over the developing world.

As a point of departure, how do government schools serve the poor? Usefully, the government sponsored Public Report on Basic Education in India (PROBE) from 1999 paints a very bleak picture of the "malfunctioning" of government schools for the poor,. When researchers called unannounced on their random sample of schools, only 53 per cent had any 'teaching activity' going on. In 33 per cent, the head teacher was absent. Alarmingly, the team noted that the deterioration of teaching standards was not to do with disempowered teachers, but instead could be ascribed to "plain negligence." They noted "several cases of irresponsible teachers keeping a school closed... for months at a time, "many cases of drunk teachers, and head teachers who asked children to do domestic chores. Significantly, the low level of teaching activity occurred even in those schools with relative good infrastructure, teaching aids and pupil-teacher ratios.

But is there any alternative to these schools? Surely no-one else can do better than government given the resources available? As it happens, the PROBE report were serving the poor and conceded—rather reluctantly—such problems were not found in these schools. In the great majority of private schools—again visited unannounced and at random—there" was feverish classroom activity." Most parents would prefer to send their children to private schools if they could afford them. Private schools, they said, were successful because they were more accountable: "the teachers are accountable to the manager (who can fire them), and, through him or her, to the parents (who can withdraw their children)." Such accountability was not present in the government schools, and "this contrast is perceived with crystal clarity by the vast majority of parents".

The Way Forward: Loosen Regulations and Set up Voucher Schemes

To many readers, the existence of these private schools for the poor will come as a surprise. It was to me too, until I had the privilege of conducting field work for the International Finance Corporation (the private finance arm of the World Bank) on a group of such schools operating under the banner of the Federation of Private Schools" management based in Hyderabad. The federation has 500 private schools (from kindergarten to grade ten) serving poor communities in slums and villages. I was impressed by both the entrepreneurial spirit within these schools—they were run on commercial principles, not dependent on hand-outs from state or philanthropy—but also by the spirit of dedication within the schools for the poor communities served: not for nothing were the leaders of the schools known as "social workers" But these schools suffer under restrictive and inappropriate regulations. One example will suffice: to be recognized a school must deposit upto 50,000 rupees (about $ 1,200) in a stipulated bank account, of which neither the capital nor the interest can be touched. Given that the fees charged in these schools ranged from 25 (60 cents) to Rs 150 per month (about $ 3.50) with most of the schools grouped near the lower end of the range, such sums are completely prohibitive.

Fees of around $ 10 per year are not affordable by everyone, but they are to a large number of poor families. Furthermore, the great majority of the schools offer a significant number of free places—up to 20 percent—for the poorest students, allocated on the basis of claims of need checked informally in the community.

All of this suggests that if one is interested in serving the needs of the poor in India, then trying to reform the totally inadequate, cumbersome and unaccountable government system is unlikely to be the best way. Instead, reform the regulatory environment to make it suitable for the flourishing of private schools for the poor, help build private financing schemes using overseas and indigenous philanthropy, and encourage public voucher schemes so that parents can use their allowance of funding where they see the schools are performing well, rather than wasting them in unresponsive state schools.

Private education in developing countries isn't just about the poor, of course, and there are many exciting examples of big education businesses. But these too have implications for the ways in which the private sector can reach the least advantaged. One Indian company which embodies much of the excite the National Institute fo Information Technology (NIIT). With its competitor, Aptech it shares just over 70 per cent of the information technolog education and training market in India estimated at roughl

Rs. 1.1 billion ($ 24 million). NIIT has 40 wholly owned centres in the metropolitan areas, and about 1,000 franchised centres across India. It also has a global reach, with centres in the U.S., Asian Pacific, Europe, Japan, Central Asia and Africa. A key aspect of NIIT's educational philosophy is that there is a need to harness research to improve the efficiency of learning and to raise educational standards.

Because of its success in developing innovative and cost-effective IT education and training, NIIT has attracted the attention of several state governments. First off the mark was Tamil Nadu, which wanted to bring a computer curriculum to all of its high schools. Significantly, although allocating about $ 22 million over five years to this endeavour, it didn't hand the funds over to government schools, perhaps in light of the PROBE report's lessons. Instead, it developed a model to contract out the service to private companies, which provide the software and hardware, while the government supplies electricity and the classroom. For the first round of the Tamil Nadu process, 43 contracts were awarded for 666 schools, with NIIT allotted 371 schools. Many of the classrooms have become NIIT centre, open to school children and teachers I daytime, then used by the franchise holder in the evenings. The contracting out of curriculum areas such as this represents an important step forward in relationships between the public and private sectors, and provides an interesting model worth watching and emulating.

Most recently, NIIT has focused on reaching largely illiterate and unschooled children through the Internet. Within weeks of having set up an "Internet kiosk" in a slum area, the institute's researchers found that without any instruction, children could achieve a remarkable level of computer literacy. NIIT is exploring ways to roll out the idea commercially, harnessing the power of the private sector to reach the poorest through modern technology.

These initiatives all find echoes in other developing countries. In each case, the private, not the public sector, is most responsive to the needs of the poor, and is bringing innovation, efficiency and educational quality to the lives of the most disadvantaged. The private sector has the potential to promote greater equity and to influence education policy, provided it is encouraged and viewed as a partner, not a threat to governments, whether in the developing or the developed world.

4

Will Education Go to Market?

The World Trade Organisation has launched processes that could open up to competition the expanding and highly protected world market in education. What issues are at stake? Most of us see education as first and foremost a public service which is responsible for providing young people with instruction. For investors looking for somewhere to put their money it is also an annual budget of $ 1,000 billion worldwide, a sector employing 50 million people, and above all a billion potential customers in the form of students.

The decision to extend to services the liberalisation of international trade which previously applied to commodities was taken in 1994. The General Agreement on Trade in Services (GATS) which was signed in April of that year included education on the list of services to be liberalised. To say outside the scope of this agreement a country's education system must be completely financed and administered by the state, which is no longer the case anywhere. However, each country can still decide freely what commitments it wants to make, and especially which educational sectors it wants to expose to market forces. The New Zealand government, for example, has decided to open up to outside competition the whole private education sector, from primary to university level.

So far, New Zealand is an exception, but that situation is likely to change. Part 4 of the GATS agreement ("Progressive liberalisation") requires that fresh negotiations should be held by the end of 2000 at the latest, and should be directed to "the elimination of the adverse effects on trade in services of measures as a means of providing effective market access". At the Geneva headquarters of the World Trade Organisation (WTO), far from the headlines and the demonstrators, work still goes on. But independently of the WTO and national policies, a number of factors are driving educational systems towards "communication".

Pressures for Change

First, education is a rapidly-growing sector in which governments are finding it harder and harder to satisfy demand, above all in higher education. Between 1985 and 1992, the number of students in higher education rose about 26 per cent—from 58.6 to 73.7 million. Meanwhile, public spending on education has tended to stagnate over the past 15 years (5-6 per cent of GDP in rich countries and 4 per cent else where).

In view of this dearth of public spending, parents and students are increasingly looking to private education for a solution. In the United States, every episode of violence in a state school and every scandal that rocks official school systems gives a boost to "home schooling", where children no longer attend school and are taught at home.

Traditional public education is also coming in for strong criticism. Employers complain it is not geared to their needs and is not flexible enough. Under pressure from economic interests, a process of "deregulating" education systems has begun. The growing independence of schools is encouraging them to look for alternative sources of funding, ranging from sponsorship to full management by private companies and including many kinds of partnerships between schools and firms. The time for out-of-school education has come... the liberalisation of the educational process thereby made possible will lead to control by education service providers who are more innovative than the traditional structures.

The development and spread of information and communication technologies on a massive scale make possible the development of paid distance learning, using multimedia and the Internet for tutorials, examinations, etc.

Secondary and primary education are also affected. More and more paying Internet sites bill themselves as alternatives to state schools or traditional private schools. The computer screen takes over from the teacher, for a fee of around $ 2,250 a year.

The WTO secretariat set up a working group in 1998 to look at prospectus for more liberalised education. Its report pointed to the rapid growth of distance learning and noted the increasing number of partnerships between educational institutions and private firms

Education for Export

Some 350 U.S experts on international trade in services, including 170 businessmen and women, gathered at the U.S. Commerce Department in Washington on October 16, 1998 to draw up recommendations for the U.S. negotiators at the WTO. The purpose of the meeting, called Services 2000, was to look at how the U.S. government should continue to support the efforts of American business to take competitive advantage in foreign markets". The U.S. currently controls about 16 per cent of the world market in services. Its services exports have more than doubled in the past 10 years and now cover 42 per cent of the non-services trade deficit.

The United States is also the world's leading exporter of educational services, and a working group at the Services 2000 conference paid special attention to this sector. It concluded that the sector "needs the same degree of transparency, transferability and interchangeability, mutual recognition, and freedom from undue regulation or restraints and barriers that the United States acknowledges on behalf of other service industries". The report said that three points should be at the centre of WTO negotiations about education.

Firstly, there should be a free flow of electronic information and means of communication, nationally and internationally. Secondly, the negotiators should tackle "barriers and other restrictions that limit or prevent the provision of educational and training services across countries and internationally." They were also to deal with obstacles to the transferability of degrees and diplomas.

Fighting for Market Share

The U.S demands are backed by most countries of the APEC (Asia-Pacific Economic Cooperation) zone. In a note in October 1999, the Australian delegation to the WTO said it would be "encouraging all members to make expanded commitments in all sectors, even the ones that have proved difficult in both regional and multilateral services negotiations", particularly education.

South Korea took a similar position. At a meeting of ministers of human resources from APEC Countries that it hosted in September 1997, the Seoul government put out a memorandum which clearly states its vision of education as a tool of economic competition.

"The emphasis on education for itself or on education for good members of a community without a large emphasis on preparation for future work is no longer appropriate. Such a view of education and work cannot be justified in a world where economic development is emphasized.

"At present, in many economies, the education systems do not sufficiently reflect labour market conditions. Their inflexible and in efficient education systems could not meet the new economic environmental challenges." So education should be made more "flexible", i.e. be deregulated and liberalised. In particular, "School systems should be established to allow all students to study what they are interested in" and "employers, with school educators, should share the role of educating students".

Some think resistance to liberalising education will come from Europe, especially France. "The future WTO negotiations cannot call in question France's tradition of public service in the field of education and health," stressed a report on the WTO.

5

Corporate Ambitions in Education

Centralization and efficiency, frequently invoking the powerful metaphor of scientific management or "Taylorism," using the stopwatch and management to discover the "one best way." These principles had been instrumental, industrialists of the time believed, in creating the industrial revolution and the wealth of powerful international companies. The quest for efficiency of those decades led to the problems we must now repair, notably the rigid and bureaucratic structure of our school systems.

Today, public schools continue to adapt new business efficiency techniques in what seems to be a constant recycling process. Scientific management, it turns out, was only the precursor to a host of ever newer management theories aimed at encouraging greater worker productivity and hence greater national wealth.

When Schools Become Levers to Attract Business Investment

These trends have echoes in the management reforms prescribed for and adopted by schools. Some seek increased efficiency through decentralized school governance while others imagine that outsourcing (or contracting) the management and operation of schools will lift educators' performance because incentives are lacking in secure government jobs.

All this is happening against the backdrop of economic globalization, which inevitably creates political tensions by pitting governments against one another in competition for transnational corporate jobs and global capital. Our current era mimics the turn of the century to the extent that international capital flows and transnational production processes influence both corporation and governments. Today, technologically induced speed, growth among investors, concentration of wealth, and interconnectedness have increased the effects of this global speculation and decreased the capacity of governments to regulate business and markets. Not surprisingly, this global market ideology has been broadly recognized as a force in national education policy.

Reforming local schools becomes one of the ways that cities engage in the global competition to provide production resources to corporations. When formal schooling is seen as a key element of productive capacity, a view reinforced by the decline of manufacturing and the rise of information-based technologies, the quality of the local public school system takes on renewed importance for business leaders and local politicians alike. Today's corporate leaders have uncommon access to elect political officials and government agency heads, the wealth of large corporations to draw upon, and the ability to affect local and regional economics simply by making business decisions.

Schools are treated as engines of economic development to lure business to a particular city or state, so corporate and local political leaders cooperate in their governance and redesign. In short, school policy becomes labour policy?

This powerful combination of corporate, national and state executives is happening at the expenses of education professionals In contrast to the turn of the century, when educators played a pivotal role in debates by emphasizing the role of schools in developing citizenship, today they have been largely discredited. Selecting school leaders from outside the field has become both symptom and spur to this decrease in the educators" status. A small but influential group of school districts is choosing leaders from among the ranks of businessmen, politicians and the military, rather than educators.

All this is taking place with little evidence that recent management solutions will turn around poor schools, nor that improvements in school performance protect against declines in productivity or the business cycle. Yet there are more troubling problems with reform strategies that pit the market against government in education. One is that education is reduced to its narrowest economic purposes. According to a 1992 survey, corporate executives most want schools to emphasize "a basic understanding of math and science:" and "sound work habits such as self-discipline, timeliness and dedication to work." These are laudable goals, but reflect a narrow set of traits that employers predict their workers will needed in an information economy their workers will need in an information economy.

The corporate model of reform pays little heed to other expectations of public schools: building just and tolerant communities, reducing distrust of one another and our shared institutions, safe guarding democratic ethics and introducing children to the cultural wisdom of the world. We are also witnessing the abandonment of many kinds of equality. Neither markets nor business ethics routinely put equality or fairness above profits. Whole groups of people will not fit the prevailing model of what it takes to be competitive in an educational market place in which competition is the guiding principle of improvement. Another disturbing trend is the anemic citizenship that economic justifications for schooling envision. Increasing the emphasis on individualism is likely to exacerbate a pattern of civic disengagement many already find disturbing in its scale and scope.

A Balancing Act to Reach a Healthy Equilibrium

We need a contemporary counter-movement to restore a healthy equilibrium of goals for our public schools. This movement would be grounded in a very different educational critique that rejects the metaphor of market (or management) failure and instead tackles the problems in our schools as symptoms of a widespread civic breakdown. The solutions to school failure would then hinge on common concerns, rather than rigorous individual competition and accountability. In addition to academic criteria, parents and reformers would craft student performance measures that reward active citizenship, tolerant and respectful behaviour, and cultural knowledge in the arts, history and languages. This reform movement, seeking equity and tolerance, would revitalize democratic institutions and not merely aim for more efficient production.

6

Promotion of Higher Education in Research

The central role of Universities in the development of skills and knowledge as an absolute prerequisite for national development is undisputed. Higher education institutions have the responsibility for training a country's high level professional, technical and managerial personnel, they are to generate new knowledge through research and advanced scientific training, and they serve as agents in the transfer, adaptation and dissemination of knowledge. Higher education institutions also play an important role in contributing to the social cohesiveness of a nation and as a forum for constructive debates on development.

In a world economy which is heavily science-based and technology-driven higher education institutions, and particularly universities, have to provide such a competence which is indispensable for building a country's endogenous capacity for problem identification and problem solution through education combined with research. In India, however, universities have so far not been able to fulfill these roles, partly because the multiplicity of their missions is hardly compatible. Many critics of the universities in India consider them to be institutions of learning and research separated from the main stream of the economic and social needs of the population which they are supposed to serve. Most of them have not managed to reconcile the missions of providing country-oriented training and research and of being part of a wider international scientific community. Higher education institutions in many countries all over the world are confronted with a large scale and mostly uncontrolled expansion of the higher education sector and the concomitant growth expenditure against a background of dwindling financial resources to support such expansion. As a result of this expansion the quality of teaching and research has declined due to overcrowding, inadequate staffing, poor physical facilities and equipment. In addition universities often show a poor capacity for management and administration. This results in a low internal efficiency which amongst others is responsible for a rising graduate under or unemployment.

These deficiencies and a lack of national resources produce dependence on external sources particularly for research development. The low capacity for planning and management makes it difficult to properly employ external sources so that there may be pockets of good quality research in one field unrelated to neighbouring areas and not forming part of an endogenous research tradition.

Measures to be Taken

The measures may be aimed specifically at increasing the efficiency of the system of higher education or of individual institutions by improving development relevance, quality and performance. More specifically are

- to optimise and diversify the structure in line with the country's development requirements;
- to improve the capacity for efficient planning and administration;
- to diversify funding sources, with the aim of relieving the state budget;
- to improve access for talented students from all segments of society, giving special attention to the proportion of women studying.

At the level of individual institutions of higher education the aim should be improve

- education and training performance in the academic-scientific and vocational field;
- research and development capacities, especially in applied fields;
- the capacities to provide consultancy and services to contractors in state, business and industry, and society.

In order to achieve these objectives, it is necessary

- to train the academic, administrative and technical staff,
- to improve the infrastructure including central facilities and means of communications and
- to increase efficiency by improving organisation.

The concept stresses the importance of measures designed to increase the efficiency of higher education in general through the strengthening of management capacities both at the system and at the institutions levels. This extends, inter alia, to the diversification of institutions of higher education in line with development needs, diversification in terms of funding, (including cost-sharing through fees) diversification in terms of study courses and practice-oriented training offered. Academic training at different levels for technical and executive staff.

New Areas of Promotion

The promotion of higher education institutions and subjects considered relevant for development (agriculture, natural sciences, engineering, medicine), the revised concept has to include areas such as the protection of the environment and resources, education, family planning and population policy.

In the wake of the political and economic reorientation taking place in many countries subjects like economics, law and social sciences are increasing in importance.

Prospects

Each country needs capacities which can produce the necessary analytical competence and research for generating information needed for designing and monitoring its development path. Institutions of higher education are essential in providing this competence. The responsibility for advanced education and the production of ideas and information should not be left to external donors. This may entail the concentration of resources, both internal and external, on one or only a few institutions of a country.

7

Wanted: A New Deal for the Universities

Higher education must meet new demands in order to turn out well-trained professionals instead of unemployed graduate. We are living through a period of profound historical change, marked by an on-going knowledge revolution. Society is changing far moré quickly than the structures it has created and the universities are lagging behind these changes. They, and the educational system in general, continue to teach the use of static processes, forecasting models based on historical experience and the memorizing of solutions to already solved problems.

Higher education systems in both North and South are in crisis, both quantitatively and qualitatively. Naturally the developing countries are the hardest hit, both in terms of available resources and levels of student enrollment.

Is the crisis due to a shortage of funds alone? Does the fact that the countries of the North invest ten times more per student than those of the South mean that graduates from the former are ten times better trained? Common sense says yes. But in most cases the answer is no. Generally speaking, university education has failings all over the world, in some cases because it is an offspring of a wasteful society, indifferent to the resources with which that society provides them.

The Missing Link Between Education and the World of Work

In the United States, for example, many teachers and researches come from developing societies which should theoretically have given them a less sound training than that provided by the immense academic and financial resources of the Unites States system. But this is not the case: they compete professionally and scientifically, with no major problems. In many areas the results of university training are comparable.

Professionals move around because they need jobs and want to work in the best possible working conditions. There are, for example, almost 30,000 African Ph.Ds working in Europe and North America, and thousands of Latin American and Asian professionals working in the United States. By the beginning of the 1990s about a million professionals had emigrated to the developed countries over the previous three decades, and the figure has increased considerably in the last five years. While the number of opportunities and access to them are uneven, there is little difference between North and South as regards quality; nor is the availability of funding the only basis for improving the system.

The problem is that post-secondary training today is diploma-driven. It is based on rigid study programmes and is changing at a rate which takes little or no account of the speed of knowledge accumulation. This is despite the fact that today's graduate professional needs to have followed a flexible curriculum and must be a problem solver, extremely adaptable to new processes and technologies, generously endowed with creativity and firmly inclined towards lifelong learning, as is clear from the studies on skilled labour done by industrialized countries and from numerous OBCD studies.

A recent study of the relationship between higher education and the labour market observes that there appears to be no connexion between the increase in professionals' level of knowledge and changes on the labour market. Although the market undoubtedly demands basic skills and knowledge, it is attaching increasing importance to the emotional and psychological attitudes of future employees.

Although post-secondary education is clearly associated with higher personal incomes, lower unemployment and greater opportunities to climb the social ladder, unemployment rates for people with higher education qualifications continue to be high in both North and South. Graduates unemployment in Europe, for example, varies between 1.4 per cent and 16.6 per cent depending on the country. What's more, many graduates are working in jobs outside their field of training. The increase in graduate unemployment in the developing countries is largely due to the drastic fall in demand from the major employer of graduates-the state-as a result of international competition and new political and economic approaches. The private sector is in no position to absorb the supply to surplus graduates. World Bank studies carried out in Asia, the Middle East, North Africa and certain Latin American countries show that graduate unemployment is increasing.

All the same, higher education cannot be held wholly responsible for graduate unemployment nor for the correlation that should exist between training, study programmes and demand for labour. It is often said that higher education is failing to provide training in the activities required by the market, but the market is often incapable of adequately anticipating the type of professionals it is going to need.

A survey conducted in Florida (USA) among multinationals in the high-tech and services sectors revealed companies that were unable to identify the professional qualities that would be required within ten years and, in many cases, within five years. This is not surprising, in view of the spectacular rise of the Internet between 1994 and 1998 which caught many hardware and software firms unawares. It is in information technology that redundancies and high unemployment levels are occurring, because systems are constantly changing and because of strategic mergers between the major companies.

Another example of the difficulty of making reliable predictions concerns those made by the European Community and the US Government regarding the type of jobs that would be needed at the beginning of the new century. These predictions were inaccurate: what had been forecast to occur after 2001 actually came about in the late 1980s and early 1990s.

It can be said, however, that professional training over the coming years will focus on areas such as high-tech electronics, information technology, aqua-culture, agro-energy, biotechnology and energy physics. Jobs in information and communication systems will require new qualifications which will have to be continually updated. The service sector will experience spectacular growth in the field of leisure and recreation because of the reduction in working hours. New professions in the human sciences such as "ludicadology", incorporating psychology, pedagogy, information science and the technology of education, play and creativity programmes, will replace the old single-discipline approach.

In short, the great occupational change looming ahead will call for increased interdisciplinarity, revitalization of the disciplines related to thick and aesthetics and sweeping changes in the attitudes of teachers and students: for the professional of the future, education will be a lifelong process, and education and work will go hand in hand.

The great challenge will thus be to create a stable relationship between higher education and society through strategic alliances with the production system designed to promote participation by all sectors of the economy in the university's basic and applied research programmes and by production-sector specialists in university teaching.

The problems of the university are also those of society, and so are the responsibilities. This raises the question of the university's specific culture, especially the teacher-student relationship. Planning is currently based above all on the teaching staff, which is more corporatist than academic. Physical spaces, salary scales, curricula, structures and timetables are more closely geared to the needs of the teacher than of teaching. This is the case all over the world.

More serious still, this teacher-centred culture is giving way to one that is even more dangerous for the survival of university education: an administration-centred culture. This would mean an education system dominated by bureaucrats and the kind of management structures which would place an institution whose function is to produce and disseminate knowledge on the same footing as a detergent factory or a multinational travel agency.

But no strategy for change can work unless higher education adapts to the challenge of the knowledge explosion. It is vital that course content should be geared to what learners "must know" and not to what teachers "know" or "think they know". This will force teachers into a permanent renal of theories, techniques and processes, keeping up with knowledge produced both inside and outside the university. Higher education is evolving towards a model in which lecturers and students will be permanent learners and where curricula will be drawn up on the basis of innovation, fresh knowledge and the latest teaching and learning technologies. Above all the university must teach people to think to use common sense and to give free rein to the creative imagination.

8

Wiring up the Ivory Towers

Prestigious universities are forging alliances to conquer a share of the e-learning market and stand up to virtual competitors Just like airline companies, universities around the world are forming partnerships and consortia in response to the pressures of globalization. The World Education Market held in Vancouver was a timely sign: the fair, expressly organized to foster relations between universities, training providers, software companies and representatives from nations with large education needs attracted participants from over 60 countries.

This race to "partner up" is fuelled by a number of factors. In most industrialized countries, government funding for higher education has decreased, forcing institutions to look for new markets either to subsidize campus programmes or just to remain viable. There is a growing need for lifelong learning as "jobs for life" vanish and the information society drastically reduces the shelf-life of almost any educational qualification. Technological developments, increasingly necessary for learners in all fields to master, offer ever more innovative tools for supporting e-learning.

For business, online learning is "the" new market opportunity with the need for retraining and professional updating predicted to crease an $ 11.5 billion industry by

2003. Business is better able to develop and maintain the technological infrastructure necessary to run large online systems and everyone, including the universities, recognizes that it takes robust telecommunications technology to deliver education and training on the scale demanded.

A host of companies has sprung up to help universities shape and package courses for online presentation, while network providers are jockeying for position to deliver online education.

The United States is the undisputed leader in the field, prompting governments in the U.K., Canada and Australia to commission being eroded by U.S. ventures turned global, Canada and the U.K. are in the early stages of setting up their own virtual universities. But what has become clear is that the conservative and labyrinthine decision-making processes which characterize most university procedures are being jolted by a race to get a share of the lifelong learning market.

So far, the most common approach for universities to break into the e-learning universe has been to develop courses specifically for a corporate partner or to form alliances among themselves. Universitas 21, a company incorporated in the U.K. is a network of 18 leading universities in ten countries.

Very often, prestigious universities has stayed clear of going fully online, seeing a danger to their brand name. Many are limiting their offerings to continuing education programmes and/or non-degree courses, and more often than not, they are aiming at the corporate market. One Company UNext. Com, has partnered with first-class institutions such as the University of Columbia (U.S.) and the London School of Economics to create online courses marketed under the name Cardean University. Their target: the Fortune 500 companies as well as individual adults. They've managed to attract Nobel laureates to design courses and the universities have formed spin-off for-profit companies specifically to develop online programmes. This facilities the commercialization of software and other products, and is a way to take a commercial approach to continuing and professional studies without compromising the University's standing.

Then there are the freestanding for-profit virtual universities which are arousing the ire of institutions that have prided themselves on a long history of public service. The most quoted examplar is Phoenix University, the largest private outfit in the U.S. Now owned by the Apollo Group, it operates the country's largest online programme with 12,200 students. The university tracks students progress and contacts those who don't submit assignments on time or fail to enrol in subsequent courses. Many critics question Phoenix's blatant commercialization, but few doubt the university's impact on continuing professional development provision.

Although e-learning is in its infancy, its impact can already by gauged. New providers are coming on the market all the time and the trend is accelerating to the point of upsetting universities virtual monopoly in educational accreditation. An Information Technology training course offered or accredited by Microsoft has undoubtedly become more valuable than a Bachelor of Science from a renowned university.

The more consumerist the approach of the education provider, the more what is taught is influenced by demand. MBAs dominate e-learning provision and IT courses are a close second. While the new consumer/learner demands flexibility, choice and just-in-time learning opportunities, suppliers will inevitably arise who are focused on meeting the demand at the expense of quality and value. And is the consumer really the best judge of what course material to choose? Education is a more complex "product" than toothpaste or washing powder. A totally consumer driven education market is unlikely to be in society's best interest in the long term. The commercialization of education usually goes hand-in-hand with desegregation: course design, delivery, tutoring assessment and accreditation may be carried out by different organizations. Students might study courses or modules from different universities or providers and then put themselves forward for examination and accreditation by yet another institution. While most academics loathe marking assignments, they regard this scenario with horror, and blame commercialization for the demise of the 'community of scholars' concept of a university. The death of the 'course' has also been predicted, with learners—especially corporate and on-the job learners—demanding short study modules. What then happens to the ability to get an overview of a field when learning consists of the students selecting a whole series of unconnected learning "bites"? Learners will be "zapping" between short sequences or presentations much as they do between television channels.

But while some faculty view e-learning with alarm, technology-based learning is where most of the pedagogical innovation is taking place in universities. Multimedia learning resources and interactive simulations are being develop for the web. Collaborative learning activities, new forms of online assessment and small group teaching technologies are making online course more stimulating, interactive and attractive then many face-to-face taught courses.

Despite "doom and gloom scenarios", most moderate observers of the scene see a continued future for the campus university, especially at the undergraduate level, while e-learning will above all cater to adult professional and independent learners. Some commercialization of education is good if it fosters innovation, concern for quality and responsiveness to consumer demands. But if some is good, more is not necessarily better! Not in education at least.

9

Shaking the Ivory Tower

Universities have changed radically to keep pace with modern life. Now where are they heading in this high-speed age? In the past half century higher education has been transformed from a privilege conferred on social and political elites to a mass activity available to whole populations. This process began in the United States in the 1940s and 1950s, spread to most of Western Europe and many other developed countries during the 1960s and 1970s and in the past two decades has become a global phenomenon. In the next half century it will accelerate, leading perhaps to the replacement of "higher education" (still an elite-ish category despite its expansion) by extended systems of "lifelong learning".

The key to this transformation has been the expansion of secondary education. For example, in all but two countries of the OECD (Organization for Economic Cooperation and Development) at least two thirds of young people now complete upper secondary education, and so are eligible to enter higher education. The result has been a dramatic increase in enrollment rates in higher education. In Chile the total number of students has grown from 131,000 in 1978 to 235,000 in 1988 and to 343,000 in the mid 1990s. Even in the United States, the pioneer of mass-acc s higher education where very high secondary ed completion rates had already been achieved before 1970, the student population has continued to grow, from 11 million in 1978 to 13 million in 1988 and now more than 14 million.

Two forces have driven up completion rates in upper secondary education and enrollment rates in higher education. The first has been democratization. As late as 1945 high levels of social, and hence educational, inequality persisted even in democratic countries, and much of the world remained in the grip of colonial and totalitarian powers. In North America, Western Europe and Australia democratization typically took the form of the development of "welfare states", in which there was an increase in public expenditure on education, housing, health and social security that was sustained over more than three decades after the end of the Second World War.

More recently, as renewed emphasis as been placed on the market even in social policy the rise of consumerism has continued to fuel demands for increased higher education opportunities. The older idea of education as a civil entitlement has been compounded by newer notions of free access to the education marketplace. Far from arresting the advance to mass higher education, consumerism has accelerated it in most developed countries. As traditional forms of social differentiation based on class, gender and ethnic origin have been eroded by democratization and by market forces, new forms based on educational certification have become more important. In many developed countries the middle class and the "graduate class" have tended to coalesce.

In much of Asia and Africa democratization took the form of decolonization. In newly independent countries the energy originally generated in liberation struggles against the colonial powers was directed into a wider struggle to create fairer and more equal successor societies. Education was central to this struggle. The result has been a rapid increase in higher education enrollment-for example, in Tunisia from barely 2,000 students at the time of independence to more than 100,000 today. That process continues.

However, the relationship between democratization and the development of higher education has been less straightforward in developing countries. Despite very rapid rates of expansion the "metropolitan" influences of the former colonial powers have lingered more stubbornly in higher education than at other levels of education. This is partly due to the continued influence of associations between universities in the British Commonwealth as well as those between francophone universities.

Partly because of these lingering "metropolitan" models and partly because levels of participation are still lower than in developed countries, many African or Asian universities have remained more elite institutions than higher education institutions in North America and Europe. Also, as economic conditions have worsened in some developing countries, the competition between primary and higher education sharpened in the post-independence years as both were seen as equally important priorities. This competition was often reinforced by the intervention of the World Bank.

The second force driving up higher education enrollments has been the changing nature of the labour market. Traditional occupations have become comparatively less significant, while new service occupations, which often require graduate-level skills, have become more important.

Skill requirements have been become more sophisticated. Jobs once done by unskilled or semi-skilled workers are now undertaken by technicians; and those which as recently as the 1980s were taken by technicians are now likely to be filled by graduates. The capital invested for every worker has more than doubled in the past 20 years. Even in occupations where there is less evidence that skills contents have changed significantly, university graduates are now employed in much larger numbers, partly to enhance the social status of these occupations and partly to compete in a graduate-dominated labour market. Healthcare is a good example. Once doctors were the only graduates; today, many para-medical workers are also trained in higher education.

The second form taken by the economic driver has been the growing conviction that national success now depends on economic competitiveness which, in the context of a knowledge-based economy, depends in turn on an adequate supply of human capital. Knowledge is now seen as the key economic resource.

This analysis may be exaggerated, raw materials are still very important in national economies and the global economy. But it has become pervasive-and persuasive. The naive and linear theories of human capital popular a generation ago which postulated a direct link between investment in education and economic growth may have been challenged; some forms of higher education are now as likely to be labelled consumption as investment goods. Nevertheless, the discourse of the "Knowledge Society" has become even more powerful.

The impact of democratization and economic competitiveness on higher education has been immense. First, the expansion of student numbers has made the cost of higher education a significant element within national budgets for the first time. A number of important consequences has flowed from this-the opportunity, and incentive, to compare the value of investing in different levels of education; increasing demands that universities are run as efficiently as possible (compromising their traditional autonomy from the state-and the market); lower unit costs as budgets have been trimmed (which may have undermined higher education's claim to represent academic excellence). Second, higher education systems have emerged that embrace not only traditional universities but also non-university institutions. Two effects have been produced. One is that the ethos of the traditional university has been eroded; it no longer stands in glorious isolation. The other is that institutional differentiation has been encouraged, whether through active state planning or in response to markets for teaching and research.

The prospects for the next half century are for an acceleration of both drivers-to include access to higher education among the basic entitlements enjoyed by citizens in democratic societies; and to "put knowledge to work" in order to generate wealth and to improve the quality of life. The prospects for higher education during the same period are also relatively easy to predict-increased efficiency (which is likely to include growing pressure to make students contribute more to the cost of their higher education); greater accountability, although more probably in a "market" than a "planning" mode as even the state redefines its role as the purchaser of higher education services, more differentiation, both between and within higher education institutions, as they struggle to identify market niches; and possibly-growing demands that higher education become more relevant as instrumental considerations triumph over idealistic ones.

However, the future may be more complex than the past. In the second half of the 20th century the encounter between higher education and society has been comparatively straightforward. Although dynamic, society has presented a familiar enough face. It was characterized by a combination of bureaucratic rationality and secular (and liberal) individualism. The beneficence of science and technology was uncontested. The dominant economic model was of large scale industry, or analogous organizations in the corporate and public sectors. Although rapidly evolving, concepts and categories like "career" and "profession" remained valid. Higher education too was familiar enough. Despite the great expansion of student numbers and its adoption of novel roles, the university continued to be recognizable as such. Other types of higher education institution have been deeply influenced by university values and practices.

In the first half of the 21st century both society and higher education may become problematical and so contested categories. Some of these uncertainties are already emerging. Once firm demarcations between public and private domains, whether in terms of the balance between the state and the market or between social "spaces" and individual desires; between producers and users; between investment and consumption; between work and leisure are becoming increasingly fuzzy in the emerging post-industrial society. Wealth is being generated by the production of "symbolic" as well as-or more than-material goods. Value is created by design, sales, marketing, service rather than by primary production. Institutions of all kinds, civic and corporate, are being challenged by the rise of adaptable and flexible organizations, made possible by advances in communications and information technology.

The force of globalization amounts to much more than round-the clock-round-the world financial markets or an emerging international division of labour; it is not only undermining nation states but also reconfiguring time and space to produce global intimacies, again with the help of the information revolution. Social identities are no longer moulded by the "givens" of religion, class and gender, or by positions within the occupational structure, as they have been since the advent of the industrial revolution in Europe two centuries ago. Instead they are being subsumed by a process of individualization in which life-styles rather than life-chances predominate.

Higher education will have not only to continue to satisfy the predictable demands for democratic entitlement and socio-economic utility with which it is familiar, but also to cope with the consequences of these new uncertainties. These may include; new curricula that emphasise style and images at the expense of skills and information; recategorization of higher education as a playful, even selfish, activity; a tighter link between experience of higher education and social esteem; submergence of the universal, but also particular, values characteristic of the traditional university by anomic globalization; threats to the scientific tradition and methods, from the "risk society", from subjectivization and from demands that other knowledge traditions are accorded equal respect.

The universities of the 21st century, therefore, may have to face two ways. They will have to continue to pay attention to the democratization and the "knowledge society" agendas, which are likely both to be subsumed in a larger "lifelong learning" agenda. Their ability to sustain current levels of public funding and to satisfy their student-customers will depend on their success in this respect. It will not be easy. There is a danger that the essence of higher education will be lost if it succumbs to unconstrained populism. If this happens, the "quality" of the university will disappear-and with it perhaps its distinctiveness and so its utility and marketability. Similarly in the knowledge Society of the future the university will face new rivals because all organizations will need to become "learning organizations". These rivals strength will be increased if the superiority of universal science is successfully challenged.

But universities will also have to address the new agendas-of the "death" of work (land graduate careers?), of new social movements (and the erosion of individual enlightenment), of globalization and virtualization (and the undermining of academic community?); of "alternative" knowledge traditions and, perhaps even, anti-cognitive values with the undermining of "objective" science and further erosion of a common intellectual culture.

10

Helping Your Child Learn

A one-syllable word begins the education process: "Why?" Parents are always trying to answer that question. And that interaction between parent and child is the basis of much that children learn.

Teaching and learning are not mysteries that can happen only in school. They can also happen when parents and children do simple things together-things such as:

- Figure out whose socks are whose-sorting is a major function in maths/and science.
- Cook a meal to learn science and good health.
- Tell each other a story as an important beginning for reading and writing; if the story is about the past, it's a way to interest a child in history.
- Plan a visit to a friend or relative for a personal connection with geography.
- Or play a game of hopscotch to develop counting and lifelong fitness.
- All children love their friends. So ask your child to describe his friend's appearance at the end of each school day. You can ask questions like. "What outfit did he/she wear?" or "How did he/she do his/her

hair?" This kind of routine query would encourage your child to observe his friend more minutely.

- If your child goes to school by bus, he can be asked to describe his route and point out certain landmarks namely colourful posters, traffic signals, large shops etc.

By doing things with their children, parents show that learning is fun and important-and that encourages children to study, learn, and stay in school.

Even on the discipline front, parents can help their children. Basic disciplinary principles must be tailored to each child and family. Before parents can become effective disciplinarians, they must first learn how to manage their own anger, solve problem situations and give and get support from others. Simple self-help techniques with or without professional support can help parents sharply reduce discipline problems.

Parents who are sensitive to their children's needs have more obedient children. Praise and love alone are not enough to instil good behaviour. Too much permissiveness hurts a child's efforts to develop self-control.

Behaviour problems should be reversed early. Waiting until the preteen-age years diminishes chances for success and puts children at higher risk for drug use and other problems.

Parents need to learn as many tricks of the trade as possible, including how to play with their children, Communicate with them, praise and reward them and also set limits for them, as well as how to handle misbehaviour using a variety of techniques.

All that parents need to help their children is a willingness to observe and learn with them, and, to take the time to nurture their natural curiosity.

11

Population Growth and Jobs

Since mid-century, the world's labour force has more than doubled-from 1.2 billion people to 2.7 billion, outstripping the growth in job creation. As a result, the United Nations International Labour Organization estimates that nearly 1 billion people, approximately 30 per cent of the global work force, are unemployed or underemployed (working but not earning enough to meet basic needs). Over the next half-century, the world will need to create more than 1.9 billion jobs-all of them in the developing world-just to maintain current levels of employment.

As economists often note, while population growth may boost labour demand (through economic activity and demand for goods), it will most definitely boost labour supply. During the next 50 years, almost 40 million people will enter the global labour force-defined as those between the ages of 15 and 65 seeking work-each year. Between 1995 and 2050, some 1.9 billion additional jobs will need to be created to absorb these new would-be workers. The most pressing needs will be found in the world's poorest nations-a sobering example of the vicious cycle linking poverty and population growth.

As the children of today represent the workers of tomorrow, the interaction between population growth and jobs is most acute in nations with young populations.

Nations such as Peru, Mexico, Indonesia, and Zambia with more than half their population below the age of 25 will feel the burden of this labour flood. In the Middle East and Africa, 40 per cent of the population is under the age of 15. Since new entrants into the labour force were born at least 15 years ago, measures to reduce population growth have a delayed effect on the growth of the labour force, highlighting the urgency of taking action on population.

Nowhere is the employment challenge greater than in Africa, where at least 40 per cent of the population lives in absolute poverty. Although 8 million people entered the sub-Saharan work force in 1997, by 2030 this resource-scarce region will have to absorb more than 17 million new entrants each year. Over the next half-century, Nigeria's labour force is projected to grow by 246 per cent and Ethiopia's will soar by 337 percent- both faster than growth of the general population. At current growth rates, the size of the labour force in sub-Saharan Africa will more than triple by 2050.

As a result of unprecedented population growth and increasing acceptance of female participation in the work force, the number of people seeking jobs in the Middle East and North Africa, a region already plagued by double-digit unemployment rates, will double in the next 50 years. In Algeria, where unemployment stands at 22 per cent, the labour force is growing at a staggering 4.2 per cent annually, and the number seeking work will more than double by 2050. Egypt alone will need to create 26 million more jobs by 2050 as its total population hits 115 million.

Nations throughout Asia will also see phenomenal increases in the numbers seeking work, including Pakistan, where the work force will grow from 70 million in 1998 to 205 million by 2050. Over the next 25 years, India will add nearly 10 million to its work force each year. During the same period, China will add nearly 6 million annually due to population growth alone, compounding the work shortages caused by the current flood of migrants to China's coastal cities and by massive layoffs-estimated at more than 30 million-as state-run operations are scaled back.

Nations are hard-pressed to educate and train rapidly growing numbers of young people in marketable skills for the global workplace. Moreover, meeting the basic needs of a growing population draws scarce foreign exchange and other resources from investments in education and job creation. Throughout the world, young people entering the work force are increasingly faced with unemployment and social marginalization. In most societies, unemployment rates for those under 25 are substantially higher than for older people.

Surplus farmland once served as a traditional source of employment for growing populations, as new land could be plowed to generate work and income. However, global percapita Greenland has dropped by half and considerably more in certain nations since 1950. Moreover, the mechanization of agriculture fuels the exodus of job seekers into the world's urban areas, where unemployment is often most acute. Heavily reliant on natural capital in the past, future job creation will require massive amounts of financial capital to jump-start the industrial and service sectors.

As the balance between the demand and supply of labour is tipped by population growth, wages-the price of labor-tend to decrease. And in a situation of labour surplus, the quality of jobs may not improve as fast for workers will settle for longer hours, fewer benefits and less control over work activities.

Employment is the key to obtaining food, housing, health services, and education, in addition to providing self-respect and self-fulfillment. Rising numbers of unemployed people could drive global poverty and hunger to precarious levels, fueling political instability.

12

Beyond Economics

Unless policymakers take a more all-round view of education, they risk sending their countries down the wrong path. Over the past decade, educational change in most countries has been driven by one imperative: survival in the global economy. This process has been particularly salient in the Asia-Pacific region following the drastic shock of the 1997 economic downturn. But in the current reform process, marked by speeding commercialization and economic preoccupations, other educational missions are being ignored, and countries risk paying a high price for their shortsightedness.

There's no denying that economic considerations are critical in today's world. Students have to acquire the knowledge and skills to survive and compete in the global economy especially one which more than ever before prizes human capital. A high-quality labour force gives nations a cutting edge in global competition. Understandably, stressing economic returns in the current educational debate attracts private resources. But education has other functions that are the indispensable corollary of more balanced, equitable development. They deserve to be briefly explained.

The first is a social function: education has a role to play in facilitating social mobility and bringing about integration in often very diverse constituencies. It is at school that children learn how to form a broader set of relationships, to live together and become aware of belonging to teach us civic attitudes, to make us aware of our rights and responsibilities—in essence, to become responsible citizens. The task is fundamental in light of democracy's advance in so many countries over the past decade or so. Then there is education's cultural function. Developing creativity and aesthetic awareness, accepting other traditions and belief systems while valuing our own are all part of the path towards fulfillment. Finally, education is a goal in and of itself. Schools help children learn how to learn and play a pivotal role in transferring knowledge from one generation to the next. I believe that all these facets of learning are critical for the long-term prosperity of our societies. In our globalized, interdependent world, these functions take on a more international character. Everywhere, education has a role to play in eliminating racial and gender biases, promoting global common interests, moments for peace, and greater international understanding.

Rising Above Short-term Pressures to Strike a Harmonious Balance

While education is widely recognized as the spine of the learning society, the complexity lies in striking a balance between these various functions. The commercialization of education that we are witnessing the world over inevitably pushes schools, educators, parents and policymakers to pursue short-term, market-driven outcomes. Lawyers, bankers and businessmen have an increasingly high profile in educational debates. Following Southeast Asia's downturn in 1997, they were influential in changing the academic mindset. In little time, emphasis has shifted from academic achievement to developing communication skills, creativity, adaptability. In and of itself, this is not necessarily regrettable. The problem is that these skills are all perceived to be at the service of a supreme economic value.

Sounder research will be required to analyze and assess where the current trends are leading us. It is increasingly recognized, however, that unless economic growth is accompanied by good governance, a fair sharing of benefits, better social and environmental protection and attention to culture, it will, sooner or later, lead to unrest. It is through education that this broad spectrum of concerns can be nurtured. Policymakers who have taken stock of this holistic mission unfortunately represent a minority in today's educational debates and reforms. Their foremost challenge is to manage commercialization, to rise above short-term pressures and to take a more ethical stance towards education, a long-term strategic view.

13

All Human Rights for All

The end of the millennium has seen some remarkable advances in political democracy. Oppressed peoples everywhere are at last, or once again, tasting freedom. They owe these victories largely to themselves, to the intelligence, determination, and even the genius of their citizens.

But this freedom will be fragile as long as it is cast in a single mold, the vehicle of a uniform globalization which speaks with a single voice, primarily that of commerce. Principles may be universal; the mechanisms that infuse life them are shaped by a host of features that are specific to each society.

No vision of democracy—which transcends politics and includes economic, social and cultural life can—really take root if it is a sterile copy that fails to take account of the history and myths, the values and traditions of each people. While these roots are necessary, however, they provide no justification for citing "cultural relativism" as an excuse for violating the basic principles on which the rights of human beings are founded. Respect for "cultural identity" cannot legitimize anti-democratic practices.

A second danger arises from the fact that the field in which these rights are elaborated and exercised is all too often limited. The recent commemoration of the Universal

Declaration of Human Rights was a reminder that human rights comprise not only political and civil rights but also, on exactly the same basis, economic and social rights, such as the right to a job, housing, health and education.

One and a half billion people live in dire poverty. Their most fundamental right, the right to life, the bedrock of all other rights, is constantly threatened. So the still unfinished struggle to extend and strengthen human rights includes the duty to promote development.

This duty is not only a matter of legal formalism or an ethical imperative. Fundamental freedoms will remain very fragile as long as poverty, exclusion and inequalities persist. The forces of globalization encourage the establishment of the rule of law, but a version of law biased in favour of rules needed for successful business activity. They also do more to sharpen economic and social tensions rather than to reduce them.

The momentum created by efforts to establish the rule of law in a growing number of countries is coming up against a major obstacle. The principles and rules that govern international relations are increasing their influence on the lives of nations, but they are very far indeed from being democratic. The strongest still hold sway.

This is true where individual states are concerned. They feel their wings have been clipped, and see their legitimate prerogatives being eroded by the rise of a kind of private-sector absolutism, which tends to limit the functions of government to security and mediation, paralyzing its role as the guarantor of the general interest and depriving it of the necessary means to apply the rule of law.

It is also true of the community of states because there is still no world structure which is accepted as the embodiment of the force of law. The United Nations is a unique international democratic forum, but its authority has been weakened first by nearly half a century of the Cold War and then by unilateral actions taken by the major powers, in defiance of the very principles they profess to defend. The rule of law is indivisible; it must encompass freedom and welfare, individual countries and the world at large.

14

Human Rights—the Road to Progress and Peace

The UN Declaration on Human Rights has been fifty years old. A moment is needed to take stock and to look at the deficits which still exist in terms of human rights half a century later. The declaration of 1948 contains a comprehensive list of political, economic, social and cultural rights and aims at the protection of the freedom, equality, and human dignity of all human beings, irrespective of their race, gender, language or religion. Never before in history had there been such a far-reaching and solemn undertaking to protect each and every individual from the all forms of oppression and deprivation. Two treaties adopted by the UN General Assembly in 1966 translate the ideas of the Human Rights Declaration into binding international law, and a High Commissioner for Human Rights, an office created as a result of the UN Human Rights Conference in Vienna in 1993, has been put in charge of monitoring the human rights situtation and coordinate UN action on it. Numerous human rights NGOs all over the world, most important among them Amnesty International, have established themselves as additional watchdogs to guard against human rights violations.

But inspite of all the attention human rights issues are receiving, especially in the Western democracies, the progress achieved in guaranteeing fundamental human rights to every individual is anything but satisfactory. It is true: with the collapse of fascism and communism, and the disappearance of many of the military regimes in Latin America, Asia and Africa, some of the ugliest tyrants who trampled human rights under their feet have gone. Democratic structures are on the advance, and with them a certain measure of rule of law. In more and more countries, governments are elected by the people which means that they are to some extent accountable to their voters and cannot violate human rights with impunity. However, even where there is formal democracy and elections are periodically being held, social, economic or cultural rights are persistently denied to large groups of people.

In Africa millions of girls are circumcised (female genital mutilation) with grave consequences for their Physical and psychological wellbeing-a serious violation of their human rights although defended by African males as cultural practice. In India, "the world's largest democracy", millions of dalits suffer from discrimination and exclusion because they do not belong to the caste system; tens of millions of children are forced to work under harsh conditions, ruining their health and missing opportunities for education; bonded labours are toiling for rich landowners in rural areas; and girls and women are suppressed by customs which still grant all the economic power to men. There are good laws in India which forbid all these practices; but the laws are not enforced in the absence of strong institutions which reach down to the village level.

This is the situation in many countries: the existing legal framework guarantees the protection of human rights as enshrined in the UN Declaration. But the reality is quite different.

All these are accounts of the daily violations of human rights which are going on in many countries and which throw a long and dark shadow over the human rights. Most of those oppressed and stripped of their rights are poor people, those on the lowest range of the scale. Because they are poor, they find it almost impossible to assert their rights which they may hold under the constitution and the laws of the country in which they live. They are often illiterate and do not even know their rights, and when they do, they have no money to pay a lawyer and to go to court. For many of the more than 1 billion people living in object poverty, human rights therefore do not exist in reality. They are far from being able to live a life in dignity as demanded by the UN Declaration.

Human rights, therefore, cannot be protected in isolation from economic and social factors. If we manage to reduce poverty, we will also help to improve the human rights situation. Development policy thus becomes a key to the problem without the enforcement of political human rights, social human rights cannot permanently be secured. On the other hand, the realisation of political human rights depends to a large extent on favourable economic, social and cultural conditions.

Human rights, when denied to people, can be a source of internal or internal conflict-just think of the millions of refugees who had to leave their homes due to ethnic and religious strife. The world would therefore be a safer place if full human rights were granted to all individuals in the world as proclaimed in the UN Declaration fifty years ago. Peace and progress would be the reward if we achieve this noble goal.

15

Speaking from a Position of Economic Strength: The Human Rights Debate and Asia

The recent debate on "Asian values" and human rights has developed into a cottage industry. At every turn politicians, academics, and opportunists of all ilks are jumping on the bandwagon giving their version of what human rights are all about and whether Asia should be unique in its approach to human rights issues and its quest for democracy and modernity. Unfortunately, in issues of this kind, the debate attracts all sorts of people, each with their own specific agendas, and neither "Asian values" proponents nor opponents speak with one voice.

What is perhaps most surprising is how quickly the debate has polarized the camps, reviving the age-old divide between East and West. Taking a step back, however, is it really just cultural differences that separate the two camps. I think the real interests underpinning the debate have nothing at all to do with questions of culture, or indeed, even human rights. Rather, they are related to Asian economic success and confidence and Asia's continuing reaction to colonialism.

I doubt very much if this debate would have even started were late twentieth-century. Asia nothing but a sea of poverty, degradation, and squalor. But it is not. Asia is booming, and economists and analysts alike are calling the next century the "Pacific Century," an obvious reference to the tremendous growth in the Asia-Pacific region. The Asian "economic miracle" has been linked to so-called Confucian and Asian values by no less venerable an institution than the World Bank. The linkage between economic growth and cultural values has given Asian leaders and intellectuals a new-found confidence in two ways. First, Asian voices, particularly those emanating from countries like Singapore, Malaysia, South Korea, Taiwan, and Thailand, are standing up to their detractors with a confidence buoyed by their countries' double-digit growth. Second, economic success cloaks many of these Asian governments in what is called as "performance legitimacy." Countries in Asia are modernizing and growing at an unprecedented pace, and Asian leaders and their people are justifiably proud of their achievements. The present Asian financial crises is temporary.

In the face of such overwhelming success, new-found national pride pits Asian countries against the "decadent West", conform to what it believes to be universally established standards of human rights practice. Constant pressure to observe human rights obligations, often applied with threats of economic sanctions, is regarded by many as a slap in the Asian face and, more importantly, an attempt by the West to hold the East to ransom. Beyond a cursory flat denial of human rights violations, Asians must justify their actions, and one powerful way to do this is by claiming historical, cultural, and religious exception. At the same time some Asian states push the cultural line to support their soft authoritarian form of governments, which have, to gather with their social and economic agendas, also come under attack from western leaders and intellectuals. In this sense, Asian states are really fighting for the right to be modern, not to forge their own version of human rights.

Most Asian scholars very keen on the "Asian values" debate because it is an opportunity to take on the West in an intellectual exchange where the West does not have a clear and distinct advantage.

The positions the West is taking in the debate are no different from those the West has always stood by. Media coverage in recent years, however, has impassioned the debate and has thus highlighted and, in some respects, shaped the divergence of interests between East and West. The stakes in the debate have come to be planted along civilizational lines that cut deep into the national and hemispheric pride of both parties. When the debate is couched in these terms, then all the other baggage is imported along with it. So I don't believe the West is overreacting in its response to the debate. I do, however, detect a sense of panic among many Western scholars and politicians-result of the fact that many Asians appear to be speaking from a position of strength; strength drawn not from the merits of intellectual arguments, but from economic success.

Can the Western response be improved? It's difficult to say. The West is primarily concerned with the merits of the conceptual arguments. While the West is concerned with whether it is at all possible to take a relativist approach to human rights issues, Asia is more concerned with power politics. The East's reaction to this must, I think, be viewed in its proper context. The problem as Asians see it is this: How can the West-especially America-preach democracy and human rights as fundamental values when the West can't even get its own house in order? Asia, on the other hand, is less the hypocrite because it takes a culturally relativist approach to the situation and does not pretend to be the champion of human rights. Such is the view of many in Asia.

It is interesting to note that the human rights debate has without a doubt attracted more scholars, intellectuals, and politicians in the West than in Asia. There are two possible reasons for this. Western liberalism and its ideals are under threat, and this siege on the Western citadel has drawn more and more Western leaders and intellectuals into the fray, compelled to stage a spirited defense against Asia's confident and well-considered alternative world view. But, it could also be true that Asian intellectuals are just having too good a time enjoying their newly acquired wealth to worry so much about such conceptual debates.

16

Safe Motherhood is a Human Rights Issue

The death of a woman during pregnancy or childbirth is not only a health issue but also a matter of social injustice. Of the human rights currently acknowledged in national constitutions and in regional and international human rights treaties, many can be applied to safe motherhood. Many such treaties and conventions are based on the 1948 Declaration of Human Rights (1); they include the Convention of the Elimination of All Forms of Discrimination against Women (2), the Convention on the Rights of the Child (3), the European Convention for the Protection of Human Rights and Fundamental Freedoms (4), the American Convention on Human Rights (5), and the African Charter on Human and Peoples' Rights (6).

Human rights of relevance to safe motherhood can be grouped into the following four principal categories:

- **Rights relating to life, liberty and security of the person,** which require governments to ensure both access to appropriate health care during pregnancy and childbirth, and women's rights to decide whether, when, and how often to bear children. Governments much therefore address factors within the economic, legal, social, and health systems that deny women these fundamental rights.

- Rights relating to the foundation of families and of family life, which require governments to provide access to health services and other facilities that women need to establish families and to enjoy life within a family.

- **Rights relating to health care and the benefits of scientific progress, including health information and education,** which require governments to provide access to good sexual and reproductive health care with appropriate referral systems. The measures needed to ensure safe motherhood can be provided through primary health care irrespective of a country's level of economic development. Central to these rights is information on a range of reproductive health issues, including family planning, abortion, and sex education..

- **Rights relating to equality and nondiscrimination,** which require governments to provide access to services such as education and health care without discriminatory grounds such as sex, marital status, age, and socioeconomic class. Discriminatory policies include requirements for a woman to obtain the consent of her husband for particular health care interventions, requirements for parental authorization which have a differential impact on girls, and laws that criminalize medical procedures that only women need. Governments are in violation of their obligations when they fail to implement laws that effectively protect women's interests or to allocate health resources to meet women's particular need for safe pregnancy and childbirth.

The actions that governments need to take to promote safe motherhood as a human right fall into three groups:

- **Reform of laws** that prevent women from attaining the highest possible levels of health and nutrition needed for safe pregnancy and childbirth and that inhibit access to reproductive health information and services such as laws requiring women in need of health care to seek the authorization of husbands or other family members first.

- **Implementation of laws** that foster women's rights to good health and nutrition and that protect women's health interests such as laws that prohibit child marriage, female genital mutilation, rape, and sexual abuse. Every effort should be made to implement laws that encourage the healthy timing of births, such as those that support the education of girls, set a minimum age for marriage, and ensure women's access to essential health care.
- **Application of human rights** in national legislation and policy to advance safe motherhood.

17

The Population Challenge

During the last half-century world population has more than doubled, climbing from 2.5 billion in 1950 to 5.9 billion in 1998. Those of us born before 1950 are members of the first generation to witness a doubling of world population. Stated otherwise, there has been more growth in population since 1950 than during the 4 million years since our early ancestors first stood upright.

This unprecedented surge in population combined with rising individual consumption, is pushing our claims on the planet beyond its natural limits. Water tables area falling on every continent as demand exceeds the sustainable yield of aquifers. Eventual aquifer depletion will bring irrigation cutbacks and shrinking harvests. Our growing appetite for seafood has pushed oceanic fisheries to their limits and beyond. Collapsing fisheries tell us we can go no further. The Earth's temperature is rising, promising changes in climate that we cannot even anticipate. We are triggering the greatest extinction of plant and animal species since the dinosaurs disappeared. As our numbers go up, their numbers go down.

These effects of population growth are relatively recent, but assertions that population growth could affect human welfare are not. In 1798 Thomas Malthus, a British clergyman and intellectual, warned in his famous piece, *An*

Essay on the Principles of population, of the tendency for population to grow exponentially while food supply grew arithmetically. He saw a world where human numbers would continually press against available food supplies.

During the 200 years since Malthus issued his warning, famine has visited countries as diverse as Ireland and India, Ethiopia and China. Indeed, despite the near-tripling of the world grain harvest since 1950 the hungry and malnourished in 1998 number an estimated 840 million-nearly as many people as lived in the world when Malthus penned his essay.

But the nature of famine has changed. Whereas it was once geographically defined by areas of poor harvests, today famine is economically defined by low incomes in those segments of society that lack the purchasing power to buy enough food. Famine concentrated among the poor is less visible than the more traditional version but is no less real.

In addition to checks imposed by food shortages, there is evidence that other checks on population growth are now emerging, such as new infectious diseases, including AIDS, Ethnic conflicts within societies, such as Rwanada and the Sudan, are also taking a growing toll. Water shortages on a scale that would deprive people of enough water to produce food could undermine governments.

The evidence gathered here indicates that the rapid population growth prevailing in a majority of the world's countries is not going to continue much longer. Either countries will get their act together, shifting quickly to smaller families, or death rates will rise from one or more of the stresses just mentioned. As human demands press against more and more of the Earth's limits, the questions is not whether populations will slow, but how. Will it be because countries do it humanely by shifting quickly to smaller families? Or because they fail to do so, and nature ruthlessly imposes its own constraints? In a world facing many challenges as it prepares to enter the next century, this may be the most challenging of all.

Estimates of future numbers are based on the latest United Nations population projections, using their medium level figures. Under this scenario, world population will grow from 6.1 billion in 2000 to 9.4 billion in 2050-a gain of 3.3 billion. The other two U.N. projections put global population in 2050 as high as 11.2 billion or as low as 7.7 billion. While the medium scenario is judged by the U.N. demographers as the one most likely to materialize, it is not an inevitable population path for the next century. Indeed, because the projections are based exclusively on demographic assumptions and do not take into account the environmental limits to carrying capacity, they should be viewed as a first pass rather than the final word on estimates of future population.

We use the medium-level projections to give an idea of the strain this "most likely" outcome would place on ecosystems and governments, and the urgent need to break from the business-as-usual scenario. The mid-level projected growth in population of 3.3 billion by 2050 is very close to the growth that will have occurred between 1950 and 2000, some 3.6 billion. But there is one difference. During the half-century now ending, the growth occurred in both industrial and developing countries. During the next half-century, the entire burden of the projected increase of 3.3 billion will be in developing countries, many of which are hard-pressed to satisfy even existing demands on resources. In fact, the population of the industrial world is expected to decline slightly.

The annual rate of world population growth reached its historical high in 1964 at 2.2 per cent, since then, it has been slowly declining, dropping to 1.4 per cent in 1998. Despite the falling rate of growth the number of people aged each year increased from 72 million in 1964 to the all-time peak of 87 million in 1990. Since then the annual addition has also declined, falling to 80 million in 1997, where it is projected to remain for the next two decades before starting to decline.

The population projections for individual countries vary more widely than at any time in history. At mid-century populations were growing everywhere, but today they have stabilized in some 32 countries, while they continue to expand in some countries at 3 per cent or more a year, Indeed, the world can be divided demographically into two camps: countries that have achieved population stability or are well on the way to doing so, and those that have not.

With the exception of Japan, all the nations in the first camp are in Europe. And all the industrial countries, The populations of some countries, including Russia, Japan, and Germany, are actually projected to decline some what over the next half-century, In addition to the 32 countries, containing 12 per cent of world population, that have stabilized their populations, in another 39 countries fertility has dropped to replacement level [roughly two children per couple] or below. Among the countries in this category are China and the United States the first and third largest countries, which together contain 26 per cent of the world's people.

Although fertility in these 39 countries has fallen below replacement level, their populations have not yet stabilized because there is a disproportionately large number of young people moving into the reproductive age group. Thus even if they hold their fertility at replacement level, population may continue to grow for several decades before it stabilizes. It was this realization that led China nearly 20 years ago to shift its goal from a two-child to a one-child family. Leaders in Beijing realized that if they did not do this they would be faced with adding the equivalent of another India to their population-a development they considered potentially disastrous for their people.

In contrast to this groups some countries are projected to triple their populations over the next half-century. For example, Ethiopia's current population of 62 million will more than triple, as it climbs to 213 million in 2050

Pakistan's population is projected to go from 148 million to 357 million, surpassing that of the United States before 2050 today to 339 million, giving it more people in 2050 than there were in all of Africa in 1950. From an environmental Vantage point, considering particularly the availability of water and cropland, it is unlikely that the projected population increases for these three countries, and other countries with similar projected gains, will materialise.

As hard as it is to imagine the addition of another 3.3 billion people to the world's population, it is even more difficult to understand the effects of adding such numbers. As we look back over the last half-century, we see that World lumber use more than doubled, paper use increased nearly sixfold, grain consumption nearly tripled, water use tripled and fossil fuel burning increased some fourfold. The relative contribution of population growth and rising affluence to the growth in demand for various resources varies widely. With lumber use, most of the doubled use is accounted for by population growth. With paper, in contrast, rising affluence is primarily responsible for the growth in use.

One way to understand the consequences of future population growth is to contrast some of the key trend projected for the next half-century with those of the as one. For example, we have seen a new fivefold growth in the oceanic fish catch and a doubling in the supply available per person, but biologists now believe we may have "hit the wall" in oceanic fisheries and that the oceans cannot sustain a catch any larger than today's. Thus people born today are likely to see the catch per person cut in half during their lifetimes.

Grainland per person has been shrinking since midcentury, but the drop projected for the next 50 years means the world will have less grainland per person than India has today. Future population growth is likely to reduce this key number in many societies to the point where they will no longer be enable to feed themselves. Countries such as Ethiopia, India, Nigeria, and Pakistan will see grainland per person shrink by 2050 to less than one tenth of a hectare [one forth of an acre]- far smaller than a typical suburban building lot in the United States.

Given that at the amount of fresh water produced each year is essentially fixed by nature, the water available, per person has shrunk steadily as a result of population growth, leading to severe water shortages in some areas. Countries now experiencing these shortages include China and India, along with scores of smaller ones. As irrigation water is diverted to industrial and residential uses.

The challenge to governments presented by continuing rapid population growth is not limited to natural resources. It also include education, housing, and jobs. During the last half-century the world has fallen further and further behind in creating jobs, leading to record levels of unemployment and under employment. Unfortunately over the next 50 years the number of entrants into the job market will be even greater. Few things threaten the political stability of a country as much as growing as growing ranks of unemployed young people.

As noted earlier, the U.N. population projections cited here are based on exclusively demographic assumptions, which are not related to the population carrying capacity of local eco systems. These projections are purely statistical, based on historical data on fertility, mortality, and average life span and assumptions about future trends.

Based on the analysis in it, I conclude that the medium projection of 9.4 billion people in 2050 which U.N. demographers consider to be the most problem is unlikely to materialize. Rather the world is more likely to follow a path closer to the low population projection of 7.7 billion by mid-century.

What is less clear is whether we will move to the lower trajectory because countries with rapid pollution growth quickly shift to smaller families or because they fail to do so and the resulting inability to manage threats from disease, spreading hunger, or social disintegration leads to rising death rates.

18

Consuming the Future

Now that we are to reach six billion of us, it is a good point to check again on what sort of lifestyles we pursue and what is the environmental impact of those lifestyles. It is curious that we have spent several decades being concerned about the growing numbers of humankind while not giving at least an equal amount of attention to the levels of living we aspire to, and how many natural resources we chew up thereby and how much pollution and waste we cause.

Everybody is a consumer of sorts. True, every fifth person scarcely qualifies for that designation, consuming goods worth less than $ 1 per day. Conversely, every seventh person qualifies for a designation of super-consumer, with a cash income at least fifty times greater. These latter are the people who, through their carbon dioxide emissions, are disrupting everybody's climate dozens of times more than the average citizen of One Earth. Fair play, anyone?

Much as the have-nots seek to match the have's, it is plain their efforts will not work out for a long time to come, at best. If every Chinese person were to consume just one additional chicken per year and if the said chicken were to be raised primarily on grain, this would account for as much grain per year as all the grain exports of the number two exporter, Canada. If the Chinese were to raise their percapita consumption of beef, now only 4 kgs per year, to that of American, 45 kg, and if the additional beef were produced largely in feedlots after the manner of the United States, it would account for as much extra grain as the entire US grain harvest, less than one-third of which is exported. Because of its recent climbing up the food chain toward a meat-based diet, China has become one of the world's leading importers of grain. The global grain market today is around 200 million tons per year, and shows scant scope for significant increase.

As a further measure of its ambitions, the Chinese government has designated the auto industry as one of five industry "pillars". Today China has fewer cars than Los Angeles. If per-capita car ownership, together with oil consumption, were to match that of the United States, China would need 80 million barrels of oil per day-by contrast with the world's 1996 oil output of 64 million barrels of oil per day. The surge in carbon dioxide emissions would be unprecedented.

All this notwithstanding, there are already some 250 million newly affluent people in China. They are people with a household income equivalent to perhaps US $ 20,000, and enough discretionary income to enjoy the perquisites of the good life as perceived by these nouveaux riches. Top of the shopping lists are meat and more meat, followed by cars whether big or small. These are the badges of success: they show you have arrived.

The new consumers in China are matched by at least 200 million in India, and tens of millions in South Korea, Taiwan, Malaysia and Thailand (the recent economic setbacks have not permanently punctured the economic bubbles). Then there are 200 million more in Brazil, Argentina, Venezuela and Mexico, and more again in Hungary and other countries of Eastern Europe, also Turkey. Put them all together and they total about as many as the 800 million long established consumers in the ultra rich countries (the OECD grouping). When the current economic hiccups in Asia are left behind, the ranks of the new consumers can be expected to rise rapidly.

But they cannot hope to become super consumers. Where would all the extra gain come from? How could the global climate tolerate the huge additional pulse of carbon dioxide? There are all kinds of other environmental reasons to suppose that environmental constraints will become all the more constraining. True, technology could help moderate the environmental impact. We could enjoy twice as much material prosperity while using only half as much natural resources and causing half as much pollution and waste. But the new consumers will want to pursue the American dream to the hilt, and it is hard to see that the best technologies could enable huge numbers of affluent aspirants, perhaps two billion people by 2010, enjoying even half the material prosperity of Americans with average household incomes of $ 40,000.

But is it true "prosperity"-mental and emotional as well as material? Or is the American dream becoming a nightmare with its harried lifestyles and declining leisure time, where the shopping mall is the ultimate Mecca, and the good life is a case of piling up goodies?

In any case, we cannot expect the new consumers to forego their "rightful share" of affluence unless the longtime affluent agree to cut back on their environmental ruinous lifestyles. It is these communities that must offer a strong example, and soonest. Where is the political leader who will espouse the new vision, however much it may be perceived as the ultimate vote loser?

19

A Crucial Encounter

Genetic tests and treatments must not be allowed to create new forms of discrimination between those who, for whatever reason, can or want to take advantage of them, and those who cannot, mostly for lack of money. If a scientific discovery can form the basis of a technology, then it is highly probable that the technology will eventually be applied. Today this lesson of history is causing anxiety among politicians, scientists and public opinion concerned about the current far-reaching developments in biotechnologies.

It is now possible to penetrate to the very essence of living things as a result of spectacular scientific advances that are gradually revealing the innermost mechanisms of life. The technologies based on this field of knowledge offer humanity for the first time astonishing powers to revolutionize the process of creating and developing human beings and, ultimately, the human species. Technically speaking, these breakthroughs could lead to the revival, in even more effective guises, of eugenic practices we hoped had been buried forever. Fortunately, this nightmare scenario seems highly unlikely.

But history also shows that new technologies are rarely applied without a framework of rules and procedures designed to ensure that they are beneficially used. Human progress has always been driven by the winds of freedom, including freedom of enquiry and initiative, but human beings have always tried to head in the right direction and to respect certain limits. The biologists have done their work: they have sown the seeds of vast possibilities. Now it is up to society to make sure that only the benefits are harvested. The biotechnology revolution beckons humanity to a crucial encounter between science and ethics.

Where human reproduction is concerned, as with technology in general, we must be guided by respect for three basic and interdependent principles dignity, freedom and solidarity.

For human dignity to be respected, each person must be regarded as unique. This position has far-reaching consequences for human procreation. First of all, it rules out cloning as a means of reproduction because this technique, which is almost upon us, involves genetically "duplicating" an existing person. More generally, predetermining the basic characteristics of a future person, notably trying to enhance their future physical or mental capacities, violates the very essence of human individuality. This kind of engineering would end up by depriving individuals of that which is theirs alone-the mysterious processes whereby their unique genetic heritage emerges and interacts in its own unique way with their environment.

Advances in prenatal scanning and testing techniques may confront parents with grave new decisions. The danger is that various kinds of pressures or even regulations will develop which only allow "genetically correct" people to be born. This would be totally unacceptable. No authority-be it political, social or economic-should be able to enact such a "genetic order", still less impose it.

So increasing emphasis must be laid on solidarity. Genetic tests and treatments must not be allowed to create new forms of discrimination between those who, for whatever reason, can or want to take advantage of them, and those who cannot mostly for lack of money.

The risk of uncontrolled, unmonitored genetic engineering increasingly looms over us. But we are starting to see the emergence of a new "responsible" form of genetic engineering in which the power of science is subjected to the power of ethics an ethics that benefits everyone, not just a few, and looks towards future generations, not just short-term interests.

20

The Trade Related Intellectual Property Rights (TRIPS) Agreement and the Developing Countries

The basic norms of free competition established in the nineteenth century induced legislators to provide relatively weak forms of intellectual property protection. Often innovators could rely only on such factors as lead time, reputation for quality and continuing technical improvements to maintain their foothold in the market.

Undermining this outlook were two developments that led to the inclusion of intellectual property issues in the World Trade Organization (WTO). First, the rise of knowledge-based industries radically altered the nature of competition and disrupted the equilibrium that had resulted from more traditional comparative advantages. Second, the growing capacity of manufacturers in developing countries to penetrate distant markets for traditional industrial products forced the developed countries to rely more heavily on their comparative advantages in the production of intellectual goods than in the past. Market access for developing countries thus became a bargaining chip to be exchanged for greater protection of intellectual goods within a restructured global market place.

Since 1986 the developed countries 'drive for extraterritorial protection of intellectual property rights has largely ignored the competitive capabilities of developing countries with respect to intellectual goods, and it has also downplayed these countries' rights to preferential treatment under existing rules. At the same time, the logic of multilateral trade negotiations skews the pre-existing North-South conflict over intellectual property rights by introducing the prospects of trade concessions in unrelated fields. Intellectual property rights constitute but one of many variables that bear on competitive capacity and the transfer of technology in general.

Primary Intellectual Property Regimes

Patents

The extension of patentability to virtually all types of technology recognized by developed patent systems, the prolongation of patent protection to a uniform term of twenty years, and legal recognition of the patentee's exclusive rights to import the relevant products could adversely affect developing countries whose existing patent laws fall below these standards. In practice, however, the competitive status of any given developing country in a post-TRIPS world will depend in part on the level of foreign direct investment it attracts and on the benefits that strengthened intellectual property rights bring to domestic innovators.

Competition under stronger patent regimes requires developing countries to adopt legal means of narrowing the scope of foreign patent monopolies and of encouraging local entrepreneurs either to work around the claimed inventions or to develop improvements suited to local conditions. To this end, local entrepreneurs should exploit technical information in disclosures published abroad; patent authorities should exercise all of the claims limitations practiced abroad; and domestic courts should strictly interpret the doctrine of equivalents. Legislative enactment of utility model laws would provide additional incentives to adapt foreign inventions to local conditions and to improve them further.

Moreover, unpatented traditional technologies will often remain suitable for local needs, and the resulting products may be sold at lower prices than imported products of patented technologies. Entrepreneurs in developing countries should also be prepared to exploit unpatented applications of applied scientific know-how in such advanced technologies as biogenetic engineering and computer programme-related innovation.

In time, increased direct investment by foreign patentees could enable developing-country licensees who exploit their natural advantages, especially low labour costs, to succeed on both domestic and export markets where non-licensees were unable or unwilling to venture in the past. Familiarization with the benefits of the patent system should stimulate greater investment in domestic research and development and in technological innovation.

The gradual extension of patents to new technologies such as computer programmes and biogenetic engineering without the emergence of agreed international minimum standards creates both opportunities and risks for the developing countries. While the developed countries enjoy unique advantages in biotechnology that only become available to developing countries as a consequence of stronger patent systems, some developing countries may find their own competitive status enhanced by the provision of proprietary rights, including plant breeders' rights, though others may not. The patenting of biogenetic advances decreases the scope for reverse-engineering and could also increase the costs of doing business in key sectors of some developing economies, notably agriculture. As regards information technologies, reliance on copyright and trade secrets at the international level appears less unfavourable to the developing countries' prospects than patents, for reasons that are set out below. However, the tendency to patent software could diminish these prospects by posing limits to reverse engineering and to the attainment of the interoperability, and this trend adds to the overall costs of disseminating information goods.

To the extent that patented technology is not made available on reasonable terms or that un-wholesome economic dependencies actually arise, developing countries will have to consider measures to restore the competitive balance that are consistent with the TRIPS Agreement. For example, the agreement allows compulsory licenses when the rights holders fail to licenses patented technology "on reasonable commercial terms". It also provides other bases for defensive regulatory action by emphasizing "the transfer and dissemination of technology, to the mutual advantage of producers and users" and the need "to promote the public interest in sectors of vital importance to socio-economic and technological development".

Measures to restrain abuse of intellectual property rights as authorized by the Paris Convention also remain available under the TRIPS agreement, which expressly empowers developing countries to deal with licensing practices that "adversely affect the international transfer of technology".

Finally, the agreement specifically preserves the right of all states to "adopt measure necessary to protect public health and nutrition and to promote the pubic interest in sectors of vital importance to socio-economic and technological development, provided that such measures are consistent with the provisions of this agreement".

Trademarks and Geographical Indications

The TRIPS provision give pre-existing norms greater specificity while softening the use requirement and eliminating both compulsory licenses and local linkage requirements. These provisions also subject the international regime of trade-marks and unfair competition to more stringent enforcement measures, including border controls against imports of counterfeit goods.

As a result, developing countries will need to reassess the pro-competitive functions of trademarks in open economies while addressing questions of abuse in a more direct fashion. They should insist on receiving the technical cooperation and aid that the TRIPS agreement envisages for the purpose of defraying administrative and enforcement burdens.

Governments should consider policies and incentives that encourage enterprises to establish their own market identities through appropriate trademarks and foreign firms to allow licensees to adapt more of the licensed products for both domestic and export needs under local trademarks.

Copyrights

Authors in many developing countries are very active in both domestic and foreign markets. It nonetheless remains true that the balance of trade in cultural goods favours exports from developed countries. This imbalance could increase under the TRIPS agreement, which generally applies the international minimum standards of the Berne Convention, plus selected standards from the Rome Convention on neighbouring rights.

While efforts to implement these standards is mandatory, developing-country authorities should familiarize themselves with the extent to which the scope of copyright protection varies from country to country, in the absence of authoritative legal limitations recognized by international law. Carefully framed public-interest exceptions may further reduce the overall costs of a TRIPS Agreement without violating international copyright norms. Moreover, the revised Berne Convention already provides for compulsory licenses for educational and scientific test, and developing countries may wish to consider making greater use of these concessions.

Ancillary Proprietary Regimes

Trade Secrets

In modern economies trade secret law regulates the pace of competition by endowing second comers with an absolute right to reverse-engineer. To operate successfully under such a regime, developing countries must realign the concept of "transfer of technology" with the nature of competition in open markets. Technology is transferred through self-help methods of reverse-engineering. The potential benefits of reverse-engineering unpatented technologies increase when advanced technologies are involved, notably biogenetic engineering, computer programmes and computer-aided design. The unpatented, non-copyrightable know-how underlying these technologies is often embodied in tangible products available to the public, which renders classical trade secret protection of doubtful efficacy. By ignoring this problem the TRIPS Agreement provides entrepreneurs in developing countries with major opportunities, notwithstanding the extension of trade secret law under TRIPS, provided they are willing and able to master the art of reverse-engineering.

Other Proprietary Regimes

The TRIPS Agreement mandates intellectual property protection for industrial designs, plant varieties and integrated circuit designs. Although the developed countries enjoy a clear advantage in advanced sectors of industrial design, more traditional sectors rooted in aesthetic appeal rather than technical efficiency remain accessible to firms in developing countries.

21

Policy Researchers and Policy Makers: Never the Twain shall Meet?

In every corner of the planet, researchers are gathering and analyzing information on vital issues of sustainable development. But how do they know that their findings will actually be used in policy decisions that create positive change? Researchers and decision makers see the world, and their roles in it, in very different ways. What creates this divide between the two communities and what can be done to bridge the gap?

'Demand-Side' Challenges: Policy in the Making

By its nature, the policy making process constrains decision makers from effectively expressing demands for research. Rigorous research requires a clear definition of a problem and the variables to be measured. But the objectives of government policies and programs tend to be loosely defined and even contradictory. Many decisions are reached through a multilateral bargaining process in which it is difficult to obtain consensus on anything more than broad statements of principle. These bargains might break down if the costs and tradeoffs involved were exposed by a research project.

Inertia and more urgent priorities mean that governments tend to think about changing policies only when time and funding have run out. At that point, it is too late for research. Furthermore, it is only after a program has been established and a clientele created that an effective demand exist for research. For these reasons, policy implementation tends to precede rather than follow research.

Even if there is a need for research, there may not be a single agency responsible for the policy decision bargaining. When a client agency does request advice, there is no guarantee that it will turn out to be the appropriate audience for the results (e.g. a study done for the Ministry of Education might find that student performance would be improve by better nutrition).

Finally, governments are often afflicted with too much information, which senior policy makers have little time to absorb.

'Supply Side' Challenges of Academic Research

Problems also exist in the research community that supplies information and analysis. University research usually takes a long time to yield results. It is often highly critical, without suggestions for action, but fitting the self-image of many academics a gadflies. In academia, a state of conflicting views and information is normal. But potential clients find their confidence undermined when two studies reach opposite conclusions.

Academics often search for general laws and patterns that reveal phenomena of greater theoretical and long run importance than highly specific observations. Policy makers, however, want answers to the specific problems they face, even if such 'small' problems do not interest researchers.

While policy makers tend to emphasize distributional concerns (i.e winners and losers) and the number of people affected, economists—frequent advisors to government—emphasize efficiency and financial costs and benefits. Owing partly to the vagueness of many program goals, policy makers tend to assess performance in terms of inputs rather than improvements in health). They also weigh losses more heavily than gains, since "a policy that hurts five people and helps five, produces five enemies and five ingrates".

Finally, the issue of compensation is critical to policy makers; for economists it is usually an afterthought. Economists tend to find a solution satisfactory if, in theory, the losers could be compensated. To push a policy change through, policy makers must usually ensure that they will be compensated, and have mechanisms to do so.

Impact Down the Road

The gap between demand and supply for research appears rather large. But this view may be too pessimistic, mainly because it uses narrow definitions of research and policy impact. Research is more than a set of data and policy impact may accumulate imperceptibly but with real effect over many years. The contribution of social science research is perhaps less in proposing specific solutions to well-defined problems, than in defining the problems and providing an array of concepts and methods for analysis.

Problem definition can take many forms. It can mean detecting problems from patterns in data, such as a trend toward worsening income distribution. It can also change the way society thinks about issues. Largely because of research, the informal sector now tends to be seen as a potential force for development, rather than a symptom of backwardness.

The most significant contribution of social science research may be in generating ideas and ideologies, which history shows can be very powerful.

What to Do?

How, then, can researchers and the agencies that sponsor them increase the social relevance and impact of research? Since both the problem-solving and the conceptual impacts are important, research programs should be designed to provide both by developing an understanding of basic behavioural relationships and a thorough knowledge of the data. This can then be tapped to provide short-term policy advice.

Donors have an important role to play in supporting theoretical research, although they are sometimes reluctant to do so. The distinction between "theoretical" and "empirical" is in no sense equivalent to "useless" and "useful". A plausible, verifiable theory about how farmers respond to increases in crop prices, or savings to changes in interest rates, is of obvious relevance to poverty and can be very useful.

Greater attention should go to publicizing findings and donors should be prepared to finance conferences, books, working papers, abstracts and the like. Researchers should convey their findings in language intelligible to practitioners, putting themselves into policy makers' shoes when doing so. Among the recommendations made by successful policy advisors are the following.

- learn about the history of the issue by researching previous arguments, interest groups, areas of disagreement and data gaps;
- get into the debate early before positions harden;
- explain which groups will be affected by the proposed measures and suggest ways to compensate those negatively affected;
- do not propose measures that are technically optimal but too complex or costly for an agency to administer; and
- Keep it simple. Emphasize the decision at hand, the underlying problem, and options to solve it. Minimize methodology, jargon and equations.

In the research domain, there is no single recipe for policy impact. Luck and persistence, along with good science, are vital ingredients.

22

Corruption: Where to Draw the Line?

Everyday the community is being stunned as reports of irregular practices compete for press headlines. The impression is that bribery and corruption, in one form or another is both extensive and increasing; although systematic statistics in this area are rare for obvious reasons.

What is corruption? The list of possibilities is extensive. It starts with the outright bribery of government officials and the more ambiguous question of political contributions; then there are a whole range of activities that could be considered to some degree corrupt-covering such things as the misuse of company assets for political favours, kickbacks and protection money for the police, payola to disc jockeys, sympathetic feature articles in return for advertising revenue, free revenue, free junkets for MP's and journalists, secret price-fixing agreements, obtaining parts in films for reasons not wholly related to acting ability, insider dealing of various kinds, as well as the improper use of the "old boy" network.

All these forms of behaviour have one thing in common. They are attempts to influence the outcome of a decision where the nature of that influence is not made public. Essentially the practices are nothing more or less than the abuse of power.

Reasons for Spread of Corruption

There are several reasons for this spread of corrupt practices. First the concentration of power in larger and larger units; particularly when combined with rapid growth where the channels of accountability are underdeveloped. It is also widespread in "mature" societies where highly developed networks attempt to preserve the "status-quo" and further their vested interests.

As Gunnar Myrdal, the renowned economist, succinctly put it in his classical study "Asia Drama". "Generally speaking, the habitual practice of bribery and dishonesty tends to pave the way for an authoritarian regime, whose disclosures of corrupt practices in the preceding government and whose punitive action against offenders provide a basis for its initial acceptance by the articulate strata of the population".

While corruption inevitably undermines the political system, or organisational structure, in the long run those involved are invariably more concerned with the short term. Also corrupt practices can be infectious. In certain areas companies with high ethical standards have either been forced out of business, or have had to give up their high standards, where their rivals have been willing to pay bribes to win orders.

It is sometimes claimed that "first class" companies are relatively "clean-at least in the narrow sense-because they can afford to be. They are already powerful and influential, with a network of informal contacts and relationships, so they do not need to beg and bribe as a way of getting business. It is often the new company trying to break into a new market, or the company fighting for survival, that is the most likely to use bribes to cut corners. Hence the problem is prevalent both in periods of rapid economic growth and change, as well as in periods of economic crisis; although there is some evidence to suggest that more of it might come to the surface, usually by accident, during the latter than former.

It is also occasionally argued-usually not very convincingly -that corruption does not actually impede development but may even accelerate it by helping to by-pass bureaucratic red-tape. However, life is rarely that simple and entrepreneurs within this approach invariably ensure that all too frequently that payments are made and nothing gets done! A recipe for disaster especially as it is somewhat difficult for the aggrieved party to complain under these circumstances.

Unfair Distribution of Income

In some cases it has been known for payments to be strictly calculated as a defined percentage of the expected gain from a legislative concession. While on other occasions payments have become so institutionalised that they are virtually another form of taxation. However, the differences between a "corruption surcharge" and taxation needs to be recognised; the former are rarely made openly, they are usually unfair and rarely are they seen to be fair. In addition they usually redistribute the income in a socially regressive direction.

The important factor appears to be to ensure that, wherever possible, practices and channels of accountability are made public. In practice, there are few absolute principle, and trade-offs are inevitable. The key element is the extent to which any decision is made openly and appears to have wide-spread support. If deals can be kept completely private, the social and political repercussions will, at least in the short term, be minimal. But anyone working on such an assumption, who then finds his, or her, activities made public, is likely to be in a dangerously exposed position.

In general, companies prefer clear and accepted codes of behaviour-for everyone. But deciding on what is fair competition, as opposed to unfair advantage can be complicated and subjective as both individual and corporate standards of acceptable behaviour are conditioned by the traditions and characteristics of the society in which they operate.

What can be done to eliminate corruption in both its monetary and non-monetary forms? The first step is usually to pass a law making at least monetary corruption an offence. It is assumed that unaccountable assets are by themselves sufficient evidence of corruption. However, there is little evidence to suggest that the extent of corruption is related to the type of legislation, as the problems of law enforcement are usually formidable in this area.

The paradox at the centre of an anti-corruption programme is that the laws must first be passed by governments and the standards set by politicians are a vital element in this process, yet these are the very people who are most likely to profit from illicit payments.

Of course no measures against corruption are likely to be effective if officials are so badly paid that they cannot live on their salaries. As a result many have combined an anti-corruption programme with an increase in official salaries. Unfortunately, although poor pay frequently drives people to extort bribes higher pay by itself, rarely stops it. This is partly due to the perennial problem that few people consider themselves adequately paid and partly because in both the corporate and political arenas ineffective control systems provide a fertile breeding-ground for the more blatant forms of monetary corruption. In order to reduce these abuses the role of independent auditors needs to be strengthened in almost every country.

It is not altogether surprising that the normal agencies of law enforcement usually find themselves unable to curb, let alone eliminate corruption. Because of this governments have set up special bodies charged with the task of investigation and enforcing anti corruption legislation. Although sizable penalties and more independent powers of inquiry are obviously helpful, it is difficult to establish any relationship between the existence of special organisations and the extent of corruption. It does not need emphasising that these agencies invariably run the risk of concentrating on the more blatant forms of monetary occupation and rarely investigate its more subtle forms. Related to this area is the whole subject of establishing a legitimate basis of "whistleblowing".

Power and Corruption

Corruption tends to be most frequent where governments take on greater powers to bestow special privileges on various sectors of the economy and society. Where there is this concentration of power there is an urgent need to ensure more open accountability. The media is frequently the key to this process of accountability but, unfortunately, it is often either controlled by the authorities, or subject to its own internal pressures from advertisers or other influences. Corruption is the universal disease of the body politic, it varies only in degree and visibility. It is least in extent when the press is free and uncorrupted and when the public are organised sufficiently to demand honest government. It is usually most widespread when the opposite conditions apply. But how often are cases revealed as a result of penetrating investigative journalism, rather than vulture like exposure once the revelation has come to light? And how often do unethical practices come to light from the systematic application of the control machinery, rather than almost by an accident?

Nevertheless, in essence, the problem of corruption is easily solved. If everyone worked on the assumption that whatever they did to influence a decision would be public knowledge, the vast majority of monetary and non-monetary corrupt practices would never arise.

Recent revelations suggest there are signs we are moving away from that utopian state. Yet, if this trend is not controlled and reversed, the consequences for individuals, companies will continue to be extremely serious. It can even lead to a crisis of confidence in the system itself.

For all these reasons it is not surprising to find that ethics is now one of the most rapidly expanding subject areas everywhere.

23

Law and Social Justice

Law reform in the service of democracy must find ways of protecting the vulnerable. Legal reform and "good governance" have vaulted to the top of the development agenda. International financial institutions and influential donors continually stress the importance of the rule of law, a healthy regulatory environment and strong and consistent enforcement of rights to successful economic development. In the new world order, the state's role is to facilitate private activity rather than guarantee the welfare of its citizens.

But there is growing concern that market reforms and globalization are connected to greater social stratification and economic inequality. What is often overlooked is that legal reform may enhance rather than alleviate this stratification and inequality.

It is important to see legal reform as a key part of a broader set of policy, legislative and institutional reforms which are designed to create not simply rule-and norm-based societies but particular types of market economies. There are no "free" markets'; functioning markets depend upon a legal infrastructure and a commitment to the rule of law. The growing interest in legal reform indicates nothing if not the widespread recognition of this fact.

Tradeoffs Between Efficiency and Equity

Respecting the rule of law and protecting rights however does not mean that there is any one best set of laws, even in a market economy. Yet legal reform projects in developing and transitional countries have become inseparably associated with the idea of single, optimal path or model. Current projects emphasize strong protection for property rights, the consistent enforcement of contracts and, increasingly, financial sector regulation as the foundation of an investor-friendly legal infrastructure. At the same time, states in transition to markets have been discouraged from adopting or retaining "excessive" regulations, including protective labour market policies that might impede growth and efficiency.

Market-oriented legal reforms can affect the fortunes of different groups in at least three different ways. The first if through the types of reforms that are implemented. Because legal reforms allocate rights and entitlements, different rule structures may well benefit different groups in different ways. In some instances, there may be tradeoffs between efficiency and equity. Strong property rights will protect owners and entrepreneurs but may contribute to the disadvantage of renters and works; environmental and consumer protection laws protect the public at large but impose costs on businesses.

Second, people can be affected by the absence of particular laws. Labour standards and laws authorizing collective bargaining, for example, have been crucial in industrialized societies. If they are weak or missing as they are in many developing countries, or if they are indefinitely postponed because priority is given to implementing laws and regulations which facilitate economic transactions, vast numbers of people can find themselves worse off than they need be in the market for labour. Particular groups may also be harmed. Women with caregiving obligations are likely to be systematically disadvantaged and shut out of better work opportunities without market regulations which ensure that part of these costs are borne by others. This is especially likely where social programmes and subsidies are reduced or eliminated at the same time, as has occurred in many parts of the world.

Open Debate

Finally, where legal reforms follows a "standard form" or are designed by experts from afar, a common experience in transitional states, the risk is that local history and priorities will be ignored or displaced and democratic control over decisions about basic social organization is weakened. To avoid aggravating inequality and worsening the position of those who are frequently already vulnerable in the reform process, three conditions need to be met.

First, conflicts of interest—between workers and entrepreneurs, for example—as well as the necessary tradeoffs that legal reforms often entail should be acknowledged openly, rather than hidden behind the veil of efficiency. This will allow countries to debate more openly the political and distributive choices that legal reforms involve. Second, donor countries and international financial institutions need to rethink the position that state "intervention" is usually or necessarily the enemy of economic development. Third, developing states need much more space, indeed they should be actively encouraged, to accommodate distributive, equity and social concerns not only through social programmes and transfers but through the processes of legal and regulatory reform as well. This would allow greater attention to labour market concerns and environmental protection as well as to poverty alleviation and gender, racial and ethnic equity.

24

On the Way to Commercial Microcredits: The Changing of a Development Instrument

The founding of financial institutions in the developing countries, whose target groups are supposed to be poorer people and, in particular, income-generating micro, small-scale and medium-sized enterprises, originated in the industrialised nations. Soon after Western "development policy" began in the 1950s and 1960s the donors noted that investment in infrastructure was insufficient to achieve growth. Reflecting on the experiences of Europe, state or mixed-enterprise development banks were founded in many developing countries with the support of various donors. The banks were to promote industralisation as a substitution for imports, as well as farming, housing construction and regional development. Their common feature was that they combined the characteristics of a bank and a public authority. On the one hand, they managed loan holdings and handled payment transactions, and one the other they "prompted" development by non-repayable grants. Since these functions each followed a very different logic, the banks were required to undertake a difficult tightrope walk.

Exclusion of Small Borrowers

As a justification for the existence of state banks, even

in liberal market economies people like to point out, and rightly so, that normal commercial banks would have scarcely any interest in the business of the "small fry" and, that they also shun longer-term financing of investment. A lender cannot beforehand tell the difference between good and less good borrowers, and must set a uniform interest rate for his credit offer. In order not to lose his cost-efficient and low risk customer's, meaning to avoid what the economists call "adverse selection", he sets the interest rate not as high as he would have to in covering his costs in the case of small borrowers, and "rations" his loans according to criteria such as reputation, collateral and business volume. Even in an otherwise completely liberalised model world, small borrowers, remain excluded from formal bank loans even if they would be able and prepared to bear cost-covering terms. That applies to an even because, other being equal, in most countries of the world they have lower incomes than men and also are discriminated against in access to property rights.

Therefore, in microeconomic terms, the idea behind the founding of development banks is well-founded. However, the design of the institutional structures, including the governance structure, requires a fine balancing of the bank and public authority functions in order to reconcile efficiency, cost-covering and the promotion mission. All too often, the easy way out for all involved is to combine the negative features of bank and public authority, meaning linking profit-mongering and the exclusion of small borrowers with a subsidy mentality and politisation. As critical studies from the 1970s showed, following the initial euphoria, development banks seldom live up to their promises.

For the donor institutions, however, these banks are ideal counterparts absorbing financial and technical assistance. Thanks to their banking function in payment transactions, they practically never have outflow problems. In addition, they can at any time produce from their broad portfolios the projects demanded by a donor or; his client, such as parliamentary committee. And promoting development banks also promotes the exports of the donors, meaning the Industrialised nations.

An important point of criticism focuses on this "hidden" promotion of exports. This is that micro, small-scale and medium-size enterprises mostly do not need a great deal of imports, and especially not so long as they are still building a trusting relationship with their bank to overcome the asymmetrical information mentioned above. So they need loans in local rather than foreign currency.

When favourably-priced foreign currency; loans are available for projects which a bank public authority or company would in any case implement or promote, these can be used for other purposes, such as for important of consumer goods or other agreeable things which otherwise could not be afforded. So who can blame politicians, bureaucrats, bank directors or companies when they prove to be fervent supporters of the financing of development banks!

Critics of the development bank system did not have an easy task in asserting themselves against the concerted interest of individuals on both the donor and recipient sides. But the search for alternatives began on a broad front in the 1980s.

Alternatives to Development Bank Promotion

Committed politicians, bureaucrats, academics, consultants and NGOs in various countries around the world began to get down to serious work in forming a new policy. Their efforts were based on the declared principles of poverty alleviation and sustainability in institution-building in promoting micro, small-scale and medium scale enterprises via the finance sector. The results were published in the World Bank's World Development Report of 1989.

In an initial step, so-called "integrated" rural and urban projects and programmes were equipped with their own "rotation funds". Which were to finance employment and income-generating measures. However, due to their integration in projects focussed on infrastructure measures such as slum clearance, irrigation, electrification, public health services and regional planning, they degenerated typically into drawing funds for projects management's. That meant that a recipient mentality rather than a sustainable financial service provider structure came into being, and the mixing of loans and free gifts undermined rather than promoted a positive attitude towards market-conform financial relationships.

The Grameen Bank in Bangladesh is a special case. Here, the charismatic professor Muhammed Yunus persuaded the government to place a state bank in the service of poverty alleviation, and for landless women in particular. The results are not undisputed, especially since the bank is still very dependent upon subsidies. But this institution shows that participation in the monetary economy is anything but a matter of course, and that emancipation of women as free economic citizens is a goal to which purely technological financial principles should perhaps be subordinated. The Grameen Bank has yet to stand the test of developing into a sustainable institution without a heroic head and without subsidies. May be it will really show now a poor country like Bangladesh can establish itself in the long term as a "funnel" for permanent development assistance transfers. But a final assessment does not appear to be possible at present.

The NGOs are another alternative to customary development banks. Donors like to promote them because they are close to the target groups, or at least are able to portray themselves so. In practice, however, they prove to be problematical partners when it comes to developing a durable formal finance structure in the interests of small borrowers. As committed left-wingers, NGO members and leaders usually take a sceptical stance towards the market and its "bourgeois" laws. They are seldom willing to act as bankers with all necessary toughness and assume the "ownership" of a financial institution.

Critical evaluations show that in some case NGOs can be persuaded to found financial institutions and also run them as sole or co-owners. But the success of such upgrading projects depends very much upon the consultants and donors, and above all upon the existence of a capable leader. They cannot, however, be regarded as a norm.

The target groups and the academics advising them on-site noticed after a while, of course, that the big words were hollow. They realised that first and foremost it was matter of the hidden agenda of the national and international financiers and not particularly about reducing poverty among the target groups. If the "frontier" of the formal finance sector was to be pushed downwards in the direction of the poor, what they really needed in financial services had to be made available to them. These were small, readily available operating funds and emergency loans and secure and worthwhile investment options for temporary financial surpluses. Since poverty was a mass phenomenon, these financial products had to be offered with a loan technology, meaning a form of organisation, that gave them a mass reach with as much saturation as possible.

The then prevailing pattern was "controlled investment loan", involving obligatory consultancy, subsidised interest rates and relatively large sums to push through innovations in the context of "pilot projects" which, however, due to limited subsidy funds, never got beyond the promotion of a few "pilots". So the reforms diagnosis meant a radical change. But there were enough people on either side of the political "barricades" who became convinced by this plausible if hardy grandiose concept. As a self-supporting commercial system which nevertheless was in the interests of the target groups, it began to assert itself towards the end of the 1990s under the label of "commercial approach" or "new development finance".

After the fall of the Berlin Wall

With the fading of utopic vision, empirically -based diagnoses gained ground and showed that precisely an unpretentious and reliable bank-customer relationship was the best contribution a bank could make to economic survival. In addition, they also demonstrated that in many cases a bank could in fact also help the target group of poor people, and particularly micro-and small-scale enterprises, to accumulate assets. Furthermore, it should be not only be mentioned but even emphasised that there were, and should be, public services of all kinds, including old age pensions, family allowance and similar transfers. Which counter poverty around the world. That was necessary to prevent microcredit programmes and similar bank services facing a demand they could not meet. Taking out a loan and servicing it with interest and repayment of the capital sum is always a burden for the borrower, and possible a benefit only in so far as it enables a special opportunity for profit to be seized. For the poorest of the poor, transfers are called for not loans and other bank or insurance services.

Development cooperation practicians on the ground and ideologically unbiased theorists alike came to these conclusions as early as the mid-1980s. But the ideological pressure did not ease until after the collapse of the East Bloc, when both the communist threat and the utopia of the non-capitalist workers' and farmers paradise disappeared.

So it is not surprising that shortly afterwards the practicians of both sides and the immediate representatives of the target groups got together with enlightened representatives of donors, consultants and academics to form an international coalition titled "New Development Finance". The Microcredit Summit of 1997 with Hillary Clinton had already leaned in this direction, even if it still sent no clear signal in regard to the issue of dependency on subsidies. But the donors gave a green light for a massive financial promotion. World Bank president James Wolfensohn promised that together with all the other summit participants he would go all to ensure that by 2005 an additional 100 million families around the world would have microcredits.

The subsequent "Annual Co[illegible]rences on New Development Finance", which took place at the University of Frankfurt—Main from 1997 to 1999, then developed into an important forum at which formerly diametrically opposed actors joined forces against the "ancient regime", According to their definition, "old" is everything which boils down to the demand of re-educating people and coupling loans with obligatory consultancy. In the long term, that results in dependency on subsidies, becoming hostage to the political games of influential national rulers and donors, and loses sight of the declared target group of the urban and rural poor. All this applies mainly to smaller countries which receive heavy international assistance. In India, Pakistan and Brazil, not to mention China, the conditions have their own rhythms and special features.

After the end of communism there was a new situation notg only in the developing countries and the North-South relationship, but also and above all in Eastern Europe. Established donor institutions such as USAID and the Reconstruction Loan Corporate (KfW) were supplemented by the multilateral European Bank for Reconstruction and Development (EBRD), and what were soon to be called "transformation Countries" lined up with the "classic" recipients of international development aid.

Internationally operating NGOs and consultancies with experience if the microcredit systems of developing countries were not also called for to assist the projects and programmes in Eastern Europe. The finance sector was perceived as the core of every market economy. At the same time, the donors soon recognised the importance of small to medium-sized business, trades, small holders and all the many disparate micro and small-scale enterprises for employment and the supply of the population. However, financial services were not available to any great degree to cover their needs.

It could now be seen that payment transactions did not function without commercial banks, and that this shortcoming had a considerable negative impact on small enterprises. Going beyond microcredits, which until then had always been the main instrument of financial assistance, the focus was now on deposits, transfers and all the other financial services that were important for the target groups. "Microfinancing" gradually became the generic term for the orientation of financial sector measures to benefit the "small people".

Downscaling" or "Starting from Scratch"

By means of special loan programmes, which were kept separate from the other portfolios, the external donors sought at first to persuade the existing banks to downscale their activities and address the newly emerging small to medium-size businesses in the private sector. On balance, the result was rather meager, for these programmes did little to influence the characteristics of the major Eastern European commercial banks. And every time some of them were privatised or had to be shut down due to financial rows or corruption scandals, it affected the special small enterprises portfolios regardless of how efficiently they were managed.

Besides using this channel via the big banks, donors also began building up loan programmes through NGOs and local chambers of commerce. The result here were also disappointing, for local implementing organisations are mostly unsuitable for a susbstanstible mass banking business.

But senior officials and executive at donors and consultancies soon had the idea of founding their own micro-finance institutes. "Starting from scartch" green field banking and similar terms began to make the rounds The first "Micro-Enterprise Bank" came into being in Bosnia and soon afterwards other Micro-Finance Institutions (MFIs) were founded.

Unlike customary development cooperation projects, which have a timeframe, the MFIs are open-ended, and consultants in the North also see themselves as long-term partner. In contrast, international development organisations are more and more becoming second-class partners from which local bodies must sooner or later separate themselves again to avoid being left in the lurch. After all, their cooperation has a time limit, and they will leave the country again.

In view of the challenges of globalistion, the banks should perhaps consider using their development projects to establish a network of long term investments and thus fulfil their promotion mission in favour of the "small people" not only locally and nationally, but also globally.

25

No Progress Without a Secular Society

Every day, women continue to be victims of rape, trafficking, acid-throwing, dowry deaths and other kinds of torture. At the opening of this new century, women are still not considered as equal human beings in many parts of the world, Religion and patriarchy continue to have an all-encroaching hold on their lives, maintaining and justifying their age-old oppression. In some South Asian Societies, this hold is even increasing.

I do not believe that there can be real equality in a society dominated by religion. Western countries speak repeatedly about the necessity of economic development to alleviate poverty. But this is not enough. Some oil rich Countries may be economically developed, but women are deprived of all rights. The supremacy of religion is incompatible with freedom of expression, women's rights and democracy. This is why I see religion as the main enemy of women's development.

We have to act on several fronts at once. First of all, improving access to education. In a society like Bangladesh, 80 per cent of women are illiterate. For centuries women have been taught they are the slaves of men. It is very hard to change their minds, to make them aware of their oppression, to give them a sense of their independence. This educational effort has to go hand in hand with a secular feminist movement in society. Such movements have to start within the country and they cannot take hold when people are uneducated and unaware of their oppression. I'm not sure you can accomplish much from the outside, except to expose in the media the atrocities women in all too many countries face in their day to day lives.

In some countries, this movement is emerging, but very timidly, and it has a slim margin of maneuver. It has the uphill task of fighting for the repeal of religious laws and the introduction of a uniform civil code. So far, it tends to be constituted by a few individual feminists who are forced to be diplomatic, to compromise with fundamentalists, be they men or women. But they are trying to change the system, step by step, and it will take a very long time. People are not yet ready to do away with religious laws that impact upon every aspect of society, from education and health to the workplace and the home.

For women's status to change, we also need enlightened leaders who believe in equality. In countries of South Asia women with a strong voice do not have the support of political leaders, whether they be men or women. Look at the countries in which women are in politics, or even heads of state. Does it follow that women in those countries are emancipated? Because of long-standing vested interests, such leaders continue to back measures that oppress women. They are not ideologically committed to changing these conditions. In South Asia, most of the women who become heads of state are religious, and like men, they adhere to the religious objectives of the Establishment. Until a society is not based on religion and women and considered equal to men before the law, I do not think that politics will advance the cause of women.

Until a society is not based on religion and women are considered equal to men before the law, I do not think that politics will advance the cause of women. In Western countries, women are educated, they are treated equally, they have access to jobs. In these conditions, their participation in politics has a meaning.

Education, a secular feminist movement, and leaders—both men and women—committed to equality and justice. This is what it will take to change the dire conditions which too many women still face today. It will take a very long time, but we are here to work towards that end.

26

Development: The People Know Best

Meetings of the World Bank and the World Trade Organization has inspired high-mined protest and, on occasion, even vandalism. But this protest and vandalism may miss the point, It is hard to blame those who complain of bullying or blundering by the great institutions of global power. But the poor of the world, especially the poor of developing countries, deserve more than street demonstrations. The poor understand better than anybody the complicated details of their own poverty—the absence of health care, the lack of education, and all the sinister perils to their own safety and well-being. They know the failures of their governments, and of international institutions.

And that is the point: it is the people of the poor countries who will have to apply new knowledge to design and achieve their own development. A country can only develop when its citizens have the freedom to address their own development problems. The obligation of the rich countries, is to give help where they can. And anyone who doesn't see a moral imperative to contribute to a fairer, more prosperous future is free to frame the obligation differently—as self-interest, for example. It will surely serve us better to invest in a peaceful and contented global community than to invite the strife and poverty of unanswered injustice and economic ruin.

Among our relevant conclusions: Powerful institutions of global finance and trade (not least, the World Bank and the World Trade Organization) can be a source of real promise to poor countries. If governed right, they can help integrate developing economies into the enriching opportunities of global trade and investment. But such promise is often wasted because the very poverty of poor-country governments weakens their ability to negotiate the terms that would serve them best.

Communities in poor countries find themselves at a special disadvantage when it comes to bargaining with foreign investors. Investment can bring growth and spread wealth. It can also threaten human rights and social cohesion, or cultural integrity, and the fragile balance of ecosystems. Nobel economist Amartyasen has spoken powerfully about the intimate relation between development and choice, the subject of his thought-provoking book Development as Freedom. Development, Sen argues, "consists of the removal of various types of unfreedoms that leave people with little choice and little opportunity..." He defines freedom as "both the primary end and the principal means of development."

A precondition of this freedom is knowledge—knowledge of the hard facts and the hard science, on which real choices are constructed, also it is knowledge of good governance—procedures of choice that are effective, responsive and democratic. For budgetary reasons, rich countries contribution to international development was severely cut in the 1990s. Now, along with others in the rich countries, they have to begin to reinvest in international development.

This means a new commitment to the improvement of lives, and to the future that the North must share with the South. It will be a reinvestment in; peace, and in our own prosperity. This remains a matter of obligation, and of sensible self-interest.

27

Social Development: The Way Forward

The idea of development is seductive; it is also elusive. It promises a lot to everyone, but it has failed to deliver to those in greatest need. In 1944 development and economic growth were largely synonymous, but by the 1950s, when it became clear that this model was not helping the poor, a focus on social development evolved. It advocates argued that economic growth as development should be pursued, but complemented with social development programmes for those who were "excluded." This approach did not fare much better, and the idea of socio-economic development, in which social development principles were to be mainstreamed in the economic growth process, was born.

Social development is commonly used to include the policies and programmes designed to combat poverty, unemployment, crime, social exclusion, ill health and illiteracy—all noble causes. But noble intentions do not easily produce the desired results; they sometimes produce the opposite. Most social development programmes, in both developed and developing countries, run the risk of fostering the victim mentality, creating dependency and deepening disempowerment, although they seek the reverse.

The 1995 Social Summit in Copenhagen, which addressed the themes of poverty, unemployment and social exclusion, was a significant milestone in the history of development. Apart from its direct outcomes in the form of commitments and an action plan adopted by well over 100 heads of states, the summit raised the political profile of social development. But five years later, while several developing countries managed real improvements in their social development indicators, the problems identified at Copenhagen are still with us and many have worsened. The main reasons for this are the usual one—lack of new and additional resources and lack of political will.

The results of the Social Summit review will be presented at the Special Session of the United Nations General Assembly in Geneva shortly. Hopefully, the Special Session will generate not only innovative solutions, but also the political will to carry them out. The General Assembly three simple and somewhat basic recommendations should be kept in mind:

- Reiterate poverty eradication as the top priority of the international and national development agenda.
- Recommend an operationally enhanced human development strategy as the practical framework for development cooperation for poverty eradication.
- Encourage development agencies and governments to use their existing sectoral mandates as entry points in a synergistic framework provided by the operationally enhanced human development framework, which could also be called a sustainable livelihoods approach.

All of the above the politically and operationally feasible. The implication of the first is to focus on the single theme of poverty eradication for action over the next five years. Social exclusion could be addressed in the strategy for poverty reduction, and employment should be seen as one of the entry points for action in the strategic action framework for poverty eradication. This provides a clear agenda around which political will, resources and action can be mobilized.

The second and third proposals addressed the weaknesses of the welfare and/or growth and trickle down approaches to poverty eradication in current vogue. Such a social agenda creates a no-win situation, in the sense that even when it succeeds in squeezing out some reprieve for workers, the poor and the disadvantaged, it produces more victims waiting to be saved an so fosters a pervasive disempowerment process. Further, and more importantly, the rationale places the economy before people.

The human development approach offers a powerful and viable alternative by fundamentally reversing the premise on which development planning proceeds—to put the economy at the service of the people rather than the reverse. The question then is how to address the social development agenda through an enhanced human development approach?

At the operational level, the following would greatly enhance the human development approach to poverty eradication:

- Begin by focusing on what people have (the assets approach), not what they need by defining assets broadly to include human, social, national and physical capital.
- Understand people's adaptive strategies to shocks and stresses an seek to further develop and release their creativity by appropriate policy, governance, technology and investment shifts and inputs.
- Mainstream the environment by giving natural capital the same level of importance as human, social and physical capital in the programme design framework.
- Mainstream gender by paying attention to different patterns of asset ownership by men and women and their different adaptive strategies.

On an optimistic note, the evolution of development practice has more often than not been characterized by a willingness to learn from past mistakes and to move forward with new and innovative paradigms. This spirit must continue if the dream of a poverty-free world is to be realized.

28

Is Copyright on the Wrong Track?

What is the purpose of intellectual property rights? Originally they were based on the principle that creators should be granted exclusive rights to exploit their works, in order to ensure they were properly remunerated and, in addition, to encourage creative activity. But in the interest of the community and of future artists and inventors, those exclusive rights were limited in time: when the term of protection ran out, the works fell into the public domain, a copyright-free space that encourages creation and competition. They could then be used as raw material and a kind of "suggestion box" by fresh generations of creators. A balance between the protection of individual property and the general interest was guaranteed.

Today that balance has been destroyed. The founding principles of intellectual property seem to be threatened by an ill-considered increase in the number of privately held exclusive rights at the expense of the public domain.

Counterfeit Software and Designer Clothes

The main factor hastening these developments is a change in the economy, which focuses increasingly on products with "intellectual added value", such as new software, the selection and presentation of information, specialized computer services, cultural and entertainment products, biotech products, and other applications of cutting-edge technologies. Control of ideas, forms, images and brands is a crucial element in this so-called "immaterial economy".

While it is difficult to steal a consignment of steel girders or a cargo of bananas, it is child's play to copy software or manufacture counterfeit designer clothes. It is easy for intellectual added value to be illicitly appropriated: it cannot be "put under lock and key". Those who want to exploit it for their own profit simply need to be able to reproduce it. Pirates in this field can market copied products at a lower price than the originals, since they do not have to pay the cost of creating or advertising the product. By doing this, they distort competition.

International Negotiations

To protect their industries against piracy and counterfeiting, the member countries of GATT (General Agreement of Tariffs and Trade, which governed international trade from 1947 to 1994) set out to strengthen intellectual property rights within the GATT framework. GATT's main concern was to protect companies from unauthorized copying and unfair competition, thus ensuring they would get a return on their investment.

When GATT concluded its first agreements, intellectual property was not very high on the agenda. In the immediate postwar years, products put on the market still consisted of atoms of matter, not bytes. It was not until the Uruguay Round of talks started in 1986 that the issue came to be discussed at the international level. That round of talks resulted in the signing, on April 15 1994, of the agreement on Trade-Related Aspects of Intellectual Property Rights (TRIPS). Like the multilateral agreements on trade in goods, the text was included in an appendix to the Marrakesh framework agreement that set up GATT's successors, the World Trade Organization (WTO).

TRIPS, which has a global application (most countries in the world have now subscribed to it), confirmed the economic importance of intellectual property rights. It requires member states to protect all forms of creation: literary and artistic work in the broadest sense (including maps and press photos). Computer programs, data bases, sound recordings, radio and television broadcasts, drawings and models, inventions of products and processes in every technological field, the lay-out designs of integrated circuits, and so on.

The agreement was a milestone in the history of intellectual property. First, its scope of application is unprecedentedly wide: anything created in the fields of technology, software, news or culture can and must be protected by an intellectual property right, in such a way that it exclusively benefits rights holders, who alone decide how it should be reproduced and distributed. Secondly, for the first time TRIPS requires contracting states to organize procedures and sanctions that enable rights holders to ensure that their rights are respected. Those states are for example obliged to allow persons or companies, whose rights have been infringed upon to go court and obtain damages. Such duties are chiefly incumbent upon the developing countries. Most of these countries do not possess the human or financial resources that would enable them to develop their own production, and they have tended to become the preferred locations of the copying industries.

A New Right to Protect Investment

Financial interests again have prompted to consider the adoption of a directive on the protection of biotechnological inventions. The move was motivated by two factors: first, "the protection of biotechnological inventions will certainly be of key importance for the Community's industrial development"; secondly, "research and development, notably in the field of genetic engineering, require a considerable degree of high-risk investment which cannot be profitable unless there is adequate legal protection".

Financial terminology—talk of profitability and an attractive "return on investment"—is invading the sphere of intellectual property. The notion of intellectual property used to be a way of protecting intellectual added value; it has now become an instrument for turning invested capital to good account. Is this a necessity or is it regrettable? The question is worth debating.

It is true that in the field of biotechnology, for example, creation requires considerable investment. This is something that industrial companies cannot accept unless they are sure of being able to make it at least partially profitable. On the other hand, one may reasonably wonder whether there is any point in creating anew monopoly on information contained in data bases, even if a great deal of time and money has gone into creating them. The idea here is not to reward an intellectual creation, however slight, but merely to repay an investment in time and money. This trend could well jeopardize the sharing of knowledge. The notion on intellectual property here seems to have departed from its basic purpose, which was to ensure a balance between private and public interests.

This change of direction is one of the first perverse effects of the exponential increase in the amount of space occupied by intellectual property. More fundamentally, it has been engineered by a society that tends to make legal and material protection the keystone of its ethos; all property and anything else of value needs to be protected against risk. Accident prevention, security, insurance and protection have become mantras in developed Western societies. It has reached the point where those societies sometimes seem to have forgotten that risk is an inherent aspect of life and freedom. The second perverse effect of the boom in intellectual property-the broadening of its scope as well as of its duration-is equally worrying.

On many occasions over the last ten years, legislators and courts have also agreed to an unlimited extension of the scope of copyright protection. Originally designed to protect works of art, copyright has been extended to cover every sphere to human creation, from the design of car bodywork or ties, meteorological photographs and the instruction manuals of electrical household appliances to data bases and receipts. Since everything belongs to someone, an authorization from the owner is required for everything. In practice it has become extremely difficult to create a multimedia work, to shoot a film, to compose a piece of music, or to publish an illustrated book without in someway having to use elements that are protected by copyright, and therefore having to request a detailed authorization from copyright holders and to pay them financial compensation.

In the short term, this increase in the number of exclusive rights will be a threat to economic activity itself. Competition, after all, boils down to offering the same product as someone else. Now if that product and all its variants, versions and components are protected by intellectual copyright, copying-in other words, making a competing offer-becomes an extremely hazardous exercise. If limited exclusive rights, which used to form part of the original spirit of intellectual property, protect companies against illicit copying, disproportionate exclusive rights quite simply wipe out competition altogether.

As for the extension of the duration of copyright, it means that the community's right to make free use of a work after it has fallen into the public domain will be a theoretical possibility rather than a fact. The present duration of copyright protection often exceeds the period during which the created work is in fact usable. After 70 years or more, an old computer programme is of no use to any one.

Similarly, the European directive on data bases theoretically restricts their protection period to 15 years, but it stipulates that if a data base is modified, notably by a large number of additions, deletions or changes which show there has been substantial further investment, the duration can be extended by 15 years. Thus, a regularly updated data base can be protectd for ever and will therefore never fall out of copyright. That contravenes the most fundamental principles that underlay the notion of intellectual property rights.

Bibliography

1. Frank Andre Gunder: "India in the World Economy, 1400-1750", *Economic and Political Weekly*, July 27, 1999.

2. Swamy, Subramanian: "Response to Economic Challenges: The Economic History of China and India (1870-1950)", *Quarterly Journal of Economics* (1979).

3. A.K. Sen: "Pattern of British Enterprise in India: 1854-1914" in *Social and Economic Development*, B. Singh and V.B. Singh, (eds), New Delhi, 1965, p. 420.

4. Perkins, Dwight H. (Ed): *China's Modern Development in Historical Perspective*, Stanford, 1975.

5. Blyn, George: Agricultural Trends in India—1891-1947 (University of Pennsylvania Press, 1966).

6. Raychaudhari, T.: "The Mid-Eighteenth Century Background" in *The Cambridge Economic History of India*, Vol. II, Cambridge University Press, 1982 (Henceforth: CEHI).

7. Subramanian, S.: A Statistical Summary of the Social and Economic Trends in India (In the Inter-War Period), Office of the Economic Adviser, Government of India, New Delhi, 1945, Table VI.

8. Stokes, Eric: *English Utilitarians and India* (Clarendon Press, 1959), page 134.

9. Brodkin. E.I.: "Proprietary Mutations and the Mutiny in Rohilkhand", *Journal of Asian Studies*, XXVIII, No. 4, August 1969, page 667.

10. Cohn, Bernard: "The Initial British Impact on India," *Journal of Asian Studies*. XIV, No. 4, August 1960, page 418.

11. Goldsmith, Raymond: *The Financial Development of India: 1860-1977*, Oxford University Press, 1983, page 47.
12. Kuhn, Phillip: "Local Taxation and Finance in Republican China" in Jones, Susan (ed): *Select Papers from the Center for Far Eastern Studies*, The University of Chicago [1972].
13. Cottrel, P.L.: British *Overseas Investment in the Nineteenth Century*, Macmillan, 1975.
14. Ashton, B., Hill, K., Piazza, A. and R. Zeita: "Famine in China, 1958-61", *Population and Development Review*, 10, 1985, pp. 613-645.
15. Fairbank, John: *China*, Harvard University Press, 1963.
16. Murphy, Rhoads: *The Outsiders: Western Experience in India and China*, (Univ. of Michigan Press, 1977).
17. In 1835, Lord Macaulay prepared a *Minute on Education* which became the basis for English language education in India. Cf *Journal of Asian Studies*, XVII, No. 4, August 1958, p. 570.
18. See Report of the Destruction of Industries in North China, Chinese Delegation to the United Nations, 1948, New York.
19. For estimates, see Rostow, W.W: *Prospects for Communist China*, Wiley, New York, 1954.
20. Domar, Evsey: *The Theory of Economic Growth*, MIT Press, 1966.
21. Swamy, Subramanian: *Economic Growth in China and India: A Comparative Appraisal—1952-70*, University of Chicago Press, 1973.
22. For details see Swamy, Subramanian: "Structural Changes and the Distribution of Income by Size: The Case of India", *Review of Income and Wealth*, June 1967.
23. Swamy, Subramanian: "Spectral Analysis of Indian Prices: 1860-1967" in Bhatt, Mahesh and Mukund Trivedi (eds), *Liberalism and Less Developed Countries*, Gujarat University.
24. Swamy, Subramanian: "Investment Policy in the Indian Economy", Paper Presented at the University of Bolognia, Italy September 1992.
25. Swamy, Subramanian: "Government-Academia Interface", Paper presented at the Prime Minister's Consultative Conference at Namibia, February 26, 1997.

26. Das, Parekh and Parekh: *India Development Report* (1999), Oxford University Press.

27. Jayal, Niraja Gopal: "The Governance Agenda", *Economic and Political Weekly*, Feb. 22, 1997.

28. Swamy, Subramanian: *Economic Growth in China and India[1870-1986]: A Comparison in Perspective*, UBS, New Delhi, 1989.

29. Reich, Robert (ed.): *The Power of Public Ideas*, Ballinger, Cambridge, Mass USA, 1988.

INDEX